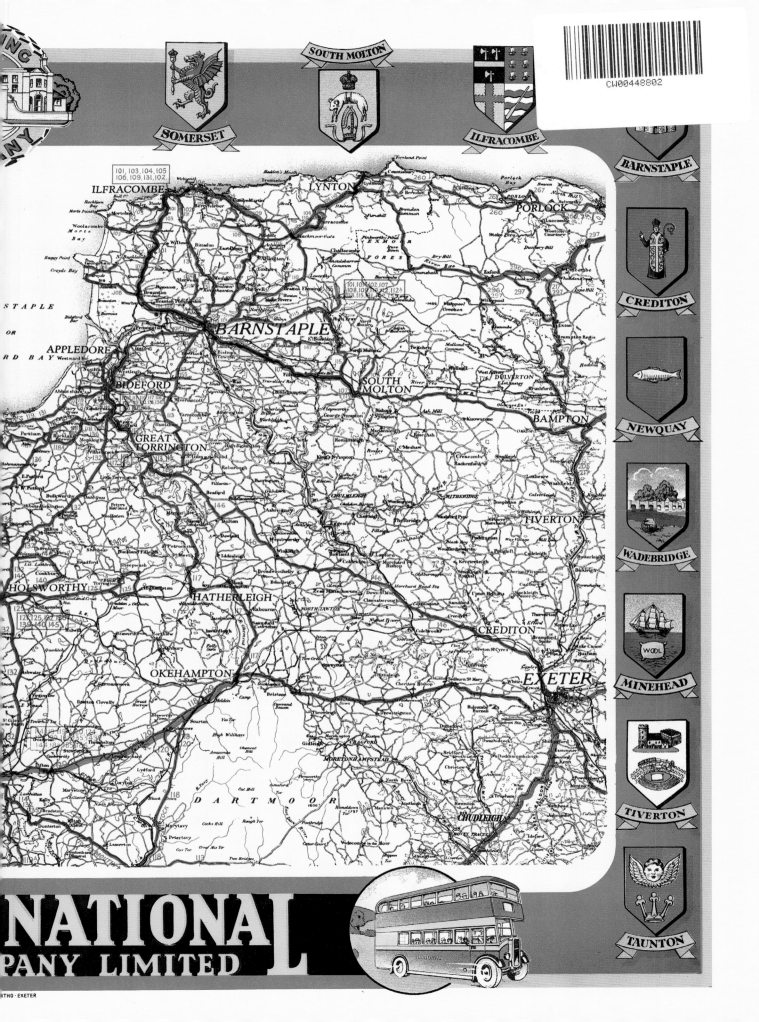

# SOUTHERN NATIONAL
## OMNIBUS COMPANY

ST. COLUMB MINOR

NARROWCLIFF
RAILWAY STATION 55

KUO 996

Ian Allan

# Colin Morris

# Contents

*For*
## ALAN LAMBERT
*Chairman of The Omnibus Society's Provincial Historical Research Group*

First published 2007

ISBN (10) 0 7110 3173 8
ISBN (13) 978 0 7110 3173 9

Published by Ian Allan Publishing
an imprint of Ian Allan Publishing Ltd, Hersham, Surrey KT12 4RG

Printed in England by Ian Allan Publishing Ltd, Hersham, Surrey KT12 4RG

Code: 0709/B3

Visit the Ian Allan Publishing website at www.ianallanpublishing.com

# Introduction and Acknowledgements

Nowhere had the 19th-century rivalry between competing railway companies provided a more marked effect upon the much later motor-omnibus industry than that fought out in the South West of England — otherwise known as the West Country. Criss-crossing and, in some cases, almost parallel lines, laid or acquired by the Great Western Railway and the London & South Western Railway, created territorial allegiances, shades of which remain to this day.

Thus, in the late 1920s, when the GWR remained the GWR but the LSWR had become part of the Southern Railway, railway-bagged operating terrain in the counties of Wiltshire, Dorset, Somerset, Devon and Cornwall formed the basis — if not the excuse — for the establishment territorially of two offshoots from the National Omnibus & Transport Co Ltd. It was a time when the railway companies involved bought their way into the existing omnibus industry.

Since the management structures of the resultant Western National and Southern National companies differed in the main by the presence of the respective railway directors upon each board, and given that the two companies shared a common address in Exeter, it has been said that the histories of both are inextricably linked. Well, yes and no! One does not have to go too far into the respective minutes of each to discover examples of outright disagreement or where *quid* was not automatically followed by an appropriate *pro quo*. It was not just the separate railway representatives who tended to protect 'their' bus company; it seems that at times the common NO&T directors were capable of donning the appropriate 'hat' and both sending and receiving the same memo upon some contentious issue or other — and dealing with it from the opposite perspective at the next meeting of the 'sister' company; a curious psychology was abroad! But, because both companies were separately incorporated with different Company Numbers, such difficulties (and potential strengths) were foreseeable.

On this basis the publisher has elected to launch two separate but companion volumes — *Southern National* and *Western National*. As Western National occupied the areas previously served by the Devon Motor Transport Co, together with its offshoot in Cornwall — followed by the large West Country area of the Road Motor Department of the GWR — it became the larger and ultimately the longer-lived of the two operators. Therefore, the outline of the founding National Omnibus & Transport Co and of the express service and Royal Blue activities of both subsidiaries are included in this, the Southern National volume, the introductory chapter being biased accordingly. Additional material will follow in a further volume, *Royal Blue Days*.

In the production of this book I have been aided, at one time or another, by numerous people. Herbert Spearing of South Street, Crewkerne, gave me information about W. Pennell King. My cousins Mollie (Churchill) Rendell, author of an excellent history of Haselbury Plucknett, of 'The Swan' in that village, and Delia Barrett of 'Montrose', Crewkerne, have helped provide background detail, as did my aunt Laura (Scott) Lock of Seavington St Michael and Roundham, whose first cousin was Tommy Hutchings of Hutchings & Cornelius of South Petherton. I was fortunate to be granted a lengthy interview with the now legendary proprietor of Safeway Services, Veronica Gunn, also of South Petherton and — many years ago — met William Harrison of Clapton.

I am similarly obliged to those who have contributed very useful information or made valuable introductions, namely: Mary Chalmers of Taunton, Harry W. Rollings, Douglas W. Morison (for notes about his father William J. Morison), J. T. Wilson, S. C. Bullock, J. C. Ransom, John Henry, Eric L. Jones, R. Keevil, Michael Rourke (MD of a later Southern National), Brian Jackson and Norman Aish. For their generous help with illustrations, I am indebted to Robert J. Crawley (Calton Phoenix) and Mike Stephens — and to my friends of very long standing, Andrew Waller and Alan Lambert. The latter, a steadfast contributor to my essays for some 27 years, personally undertook a considerable amount of research on my behalf, the results of which are incorporated within this volume. For that reason, this book is dedicated gratefully to him.

**Note:** Those who wish to study detailed notes upon the rolling stock, services, acquired operators, senior officers and premises are directed to *The Years Between — 1909-1969, Vol 1: The National Story* and *Vol 3: The Story of Western National and Southern National* (1979 and 1990 respectively) by R. J. Crawley *et al.*

# CHAPTER ONE

# The National Omnibus & Transport Co Ltd

The first 'large-capacity' road passenger transport to operate without the use of horse or rails, in what was to become part of the National company's area, was this steam-driven 'road train'. Built by the Liquid Fuel Engineering Co Ltd, the 35hp tractor/van and its 20-seated trailer ran at Cirencester in 1897, in connection with the Midland & South Western Junction and Great Western railways. *Alan Lambert collection*

THE histories of National's operational subsidiary companies — Western National, Southern National and Eastern National — have a somewhat different starting point from those other territorial omnibus firms whose fleet identities were once household names in the United Kingdom. Like many of them, it was the initial drive of a single-minded individual which first put National upon the road, but in this case the founder proved to be more interested in the development of the vehicles themselves rather than the potential for territorial expansion which a rival form of propulsion could provide.

Thomas Clarkson was an engineer of the old school. The Industrial Revolution had been founded upon the power of steam. If ships, railway locomotives, traction and ploughing engines and machinery for mass-production could be successfully operated by harnessing boiled water under pressure, so too could road passenger transport. Sir Goldsworthy Gurney (1826), Walter Hancock (1835) and others since had proved that the idea worked in principle. What was needed was a systematic improvement of each component part involved. Clarkson set out to devote his energies to doing just that. If his impressive work had succeeded long-term, the British bus industry — during its formative years, at the very least — might well have been powered by paraffin and water.

In the latter years of the 19th century Clarkson was not alone in his work with steam-driven passenger-carrying road vehicles. The Liquid Fuel Engineering Co Ltd, based at Cowes on the Isle of Wight (and employing a young man who would later join National's ranks), produced steam-driven wagonettes, a tram and goods/passenger combinations, all of which seem to have featured the familiar 'traction engine'-style chimney to vent the products of combustion — an arrangement which, save for one 'coke-motor' example, Clarkson managed to eschew.

A LIFU, however, was the first passenger-carrying vehicle to be employed on a route destined to become National territory in the South West of England. The LIFU steam motor road train was built to the design of the company's Works Manager, H. A. House Jr, to run between Cirencester and Fairford (Gloucestershire) in connection with the Midland & South Western Junction and Great Western railways. The tractor unit was a steam van capable of carrying up to 3 tons of goods, coupled to a passenger-carrying trailer with 20 seats arranged wagonette-fashion inside an enclosed omnibus — combined length 35ft. The tractor, which was tiller-steered, had two 20-gallon oil tanks and carried 85 gallons of water. This gave the road train a range of 15 miles — awkward perhaps, for the distance between Cirencester and

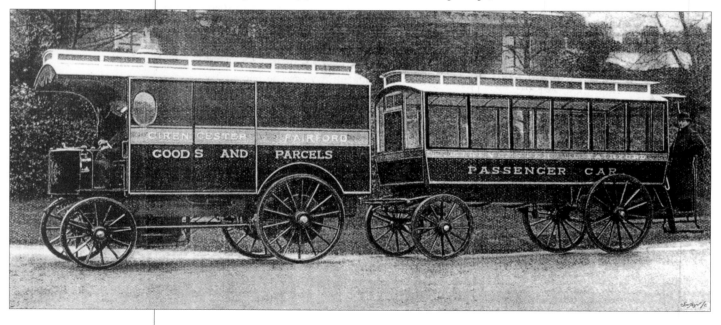

CIRENCESTER — FAIRFORD
GOODS AND PARCELS

PASSENGER CAR

Fairford was eight miles. The combination, whose speed hovered between six and eight growling miles per hour, began what turned out to be a trial operation in November 1897.

Clarkson's approach to the design problem was altogether more sophisticated and, visually at least, owed much to the emergent vehicles powered by an internal-combustion engine. Following the production of an elegant steam-powered landau, in 1902 he moved his manufacturing premises from London to the Moulsham Works in Chelmsford, Essex. Here he built an extremely neat and tidy steam-driven light car, which was exhibited at the 1903 Automobile Show.

Among the visitors to the exhibition was an influential party from Torquay, which led to that resort's providing a considerable kick-start to his popularity as a manufacturer. Between 1903 and 1905 — well before trams appeared in the town (see *Glory Days: Devon General*)— the Torquay & District Motor Omnibus Co received eight enlarged versions of the 1903 exhibition car, seating between 15 and 20. A similar pair, delivered originally to the Cirencester Motor Omnibus Co, turned up in Torbay to work second-hand for R. Coombes' Paignton & District Motor Omnibus Co, while in 1907 the Torquay Road Car Co Ltd ran eight, bought from the Great Western Railway and the Vale of Llangollen Engineering Bus & Garage Co Ltd (two of those being ex-Sussex Motor Road Car Co Ltd). The Torquay–Chelston Steam Car Co Ltd was to purchase a Clarkson Chelmsford IV as late as July 1911.

The most impressive Clarksons — in terms of appearance, if not reliability — were four 32hp steam buses delivered to the London & South Western Railway in 1905. Fitted with Munnion bodywork, which although single-deck was of cathedral-like proportion, these were employed at one stage in Devon, on a route between Exeter and Chagford. By this date Clarkson steamers were at work nationwide and in several parts of the British Empire. The ex-GWR vehicles mentioned above had previously run from Bridgwater to North Petherton and to Stogursey — two other services that were destined to become part of the National route system in the West Country.

Much of the transferring of these early vehicles from one place to another had to do with the boilers' ability or otherwise to cope with the local water supply. This was one factor which contributed toward batches tried by the London General Omnibus Co, the London Road Car Co and several smaller operators in the metropolis being rejected in favour of vehicles with internal-combustion engines. These became desperate times for Clarkson, who realised that double-deck vehicles would in any case be necessary to move sufficient passengers at one go.

The breakthrough came in three stages. First, at a time when the military was beginning to take a serious interest in mechanical traction (following, ironically, the success of Thornycroft-built traction engines in the Boer War), Thomas Clarkson seized the chance, in December 1908, to drive five bus-loads of Essex Yeomanry Territorials with full equipment some 14 miles in pouring rain from Chelmsford to Latchington in 1hr 18min. Colonel R. B. Colvin of the Essex Yeomanry was most impressed — the nation was safe from invasion if troops could be rushed so quickly to points not served by the railways. He subsequently requested the use of four double-deckers to take his Territorials to camp in May 1909.

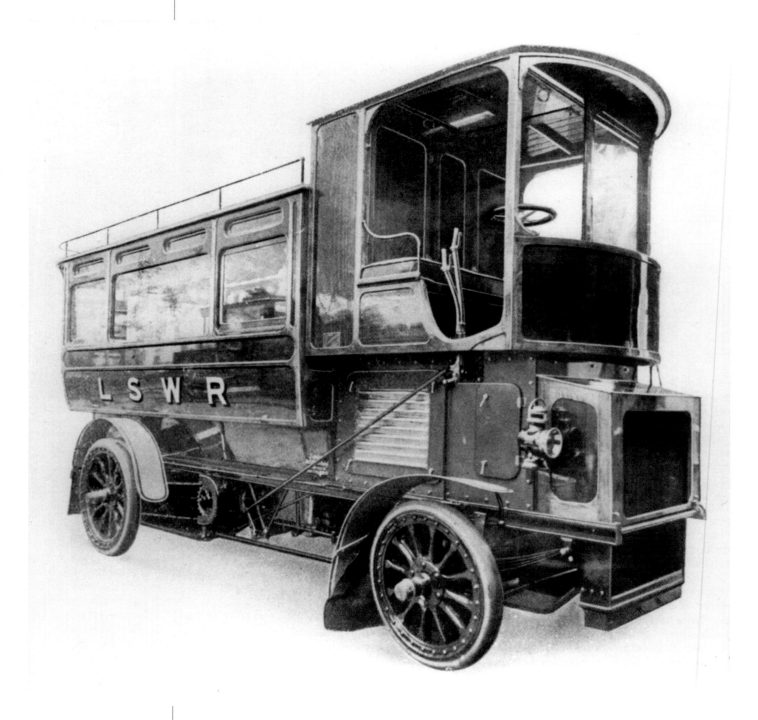

The London & South Western Railway ran some Clarkson steamers of cathedral-like proportion between Exeter and Chagford but was obliged by their foibles to replace them. The problems began early. Given the task of driving from the works, the young William Morison discovered that he had to steer in the opposite direction from the one intended. That, at least, was put right before it arrived in Devon.
*Colin Morris collection*

In an inspirational moment Clarkson chose to attract as much publicity as possible during this contract by painting the buses white and gold — and had them labelled 'NATIONAL' on both sides to emphasise his contribution to the nation's security. It was an exercise exactly concurrent with the provision of Worthing Motor Services vehicles for the Sussex Royal Garrison Artillery's 'Motor Dash' from Brighton to Newhaven Fort, but with petrol-engined buses. For once, however, Douglas Mackenzie, of WMS and later Southdown fame, failed to capitalise fully upon his equally pioneering contribution to military mobility. Clarkson, on the other hand, had created a stylish fleetname, echoes of which survive the best part of a century later.

Afterward frustrated by insufficient sales of his steam-powered vehicles, Clarkson took the bold decision to launch his own bus company and set up a network of routes where traffic was at its greatest — in London. This was done with the advice and help of his friend Colonel Colvin and the monetary participation of the Liverpool Mortgage Insurance Co, which at that stage owned a large proportion of the Chelmsford-based Moulsham Works and patents. The National Steam Car Company was launched in October 1909 and began running its first route — from Shepherd's Bush to Lambeth

North — the following month. The service was extended and the company reconstituted as the National Steam Car Co (1911) Ltd on 27 March 1911. Shepherd's Bush depot was to become an aspect of the National company's activities which have a bearing upon the content of this book (see below and Chapter 5).

It is perhaps appropriate to record here that by 1919, when the National Steam Car Co Ltd came to a 'withdrawal to the provinces' agreement in favour of the London General Omnibus Co Ltd, National's London routes had extended to Hornsey, Tottenham and Stoke Newington in the north, Hounslow, Teddington and Hampton Court in the west, Dulwich in the south and Bexley in the east, with a pretty-well standardised fleet of 34-seat open-top double-decked Clarksons — almost 200 of them when it had stepped in to replace LGOC B types sent for World War 1 service in France.

What also requires noting here is that in July 1913 the company negotiated the purchase of the Chelmsford-based bus services of the Great Eastern Railway and ran Clarksons to some nine destinations from a base in Viaduct Road, Chelmsford. To this acquisition may be traced the origins of the later Eastern National Omnibus Co Ltd. (See *Glory Days: Eastern National* by Richard Delahoy).

Thomas Clarkson's first double-deck steam-powered omnibus — a demonstrator — was built in 1907 and began its road work the following year. Fitted with open-topped bodywork by the Gloucester Carriage & Wagon Works Ltd, F 2582 was a 34-seater. The design of the lower-deck saloon was based upon Christopher Dodson's 'railway type'.
*Oxford Publishing Co*

In 1914, with the cost of petrol rising considerably, Thomas Clarkson launched his 'National Coke Motor'. Although the buses of the National Steam Car Co normally ran on paraffin (and water), he fitted No 194 (F 8512) with his National coke-fired steam engine. Here it is on a seven-day trial at Brighton in January 1915. No 194, like all its paraffin-fired double-deck fellows, was a 34-seater.
*Alan Lambert collection*

In 1917 Thomas Clarkson, head down, developing an advanced steam chassis, was replaced as Chairman by K. P. Hawksley, a consulting engineer. Under his chairmanship National appointed Walter James Iden as 'Joint Managing Director' together with Thomas Clarkson in a similarly described role — an uneasy pairing. Iden had considerable experience in the omnibus industry and in heavy motor engineering. His posts had included being Chief Engineer at LGOC, Manager of the Associated Equipment Company (AEC) at Walthamstow and Manager of Crossley Motors Ltd of Manchester.

It was at this point that three other names of considerable importance to the National story rose to prominence. Bert Smith, originally Secretary in 1912, resumed in that post and was appointed additionally Traffic Manager in 1918; John J. Jarvis joined the board destined to oversee the affairs of the company and its later operating subsidiaries until a takeover by Tilling in 1932, while William J. Morison, co-author with Thomas Clarkson of

several patented company inventions, was destined to become Chief Engineer.

The parting of the ways between the 'joint managing directors' came in the summer of 1918, five months before World War 1 drew to a close. Thomas Clarkson had just put the finishing touches to his new steam chassis, which he saw as the future fleet-replacement vehicle. However, W. J. Iden managed to convince the board that the company's future lay with the petrol-fired internal-combustion engine, and in August 1919 AEC YC buses and charabancs began entering service with National.

That was the year that National withdrew its Central London routes 'to concentrate upon provincial services'. As a tempter the LGOC had successfully offered National its Bedford garage and its attendant services — an area then detached by some 14 miles from National's Essex operations. National, however, was permitted to keep its garage at Shepherd's Bush, that it might continue on a limited scale its London-based private hires and excursions.

| | | | | | | | | | Unit Nos. | | | | | | |
|---|---|---|---|---|---|---|---|---|---|---|---|---|---|---|---|
| Date | Route | Fuel Used. | Miles Run. | Miles Lost. | M.P.G. Fuel. | Invol. Stops. | Lub. Oil. | M.P.G. Lub. | Engine | Rear Axle. | Front Axle. | Stg. | Diff. | Gear Box. | Remarks. | Driver's Name |

THE NATIONAL STEAM CAR CO., LTD.
CAR RECORD.

Garage_____
Date when Licensed_____
Form No. 48. H. C. & Co. 9050. 5m. 7/19.

Chassis No._____
Car No._____
Registered No._____
L.C.C. No._____

VEHICLE FAILURES involving
FAILED VEHICLES.

THE NATIONAL STEAM CAR CO., LTD.
DRIVER'S MECHANICAL REPORTS.

*Left:* National acquired its Edward Street, Weymouth, property in March 1925, when it purchased the business of the Weymouth Motor Co Ltd for £6,200. Among the nine charabancs that passed to National was this Daimler CK 30-seater (FX 7322), which became No 2223 in the National fleet. When the company was divided into three operational companies it departed from Weymouth to join Eastern National. *Alan Lambert collection*

*Below left:* Operated by Road Motors Ltd's Weymouth branch, established in 1921, this Palladium 40hp double-decker was photographed at the Royal Oak, Upwey, terminus of its journey from Radipole and the King's Statue. No 15 (NM 462) in the Road Motors fleet, this 40-seater became No 2251 with the National Omnibus & Transport Co Ltd in 1925, National having purchased both the Luton and Weymouth branches of RML. *Alan Lambert collection*

The National Omnibus & Transport Company Ltd.
**TOTAL WAY BILL**

THE NATIONAL OMNIBUS AND TRANSPORT COMPANY, LIMITED.

*Left:* Just prior to the formation of Colwills (Ilfracombe) Ltd, Capt Shiers — still in uniform — has arrived and collected a full load of passengers from Colwills' office. They look very happy at the prospect of a 'Motor Trip'. Laura Colwill stands in the doorway to see them off. The vehicle (TA 7082), an AEC YC, is Shiers' own. *Alan Lambert collection*

*Right:* Laura Colwill watches as a Colwills (Ilfracombe) Ltd stage-carriage bus is momentarily posed, passengers and all, outside her office. This vehicle, Daimler CK No 3 (FM 1434), with Eaton bodywork, is painted in the dove-grey livery of Crosville, Chester (where it was registered), and has its fleetname and fleet number applied in pure Crosville style also. *Alan Lambert collection*

*Right:* In keeping with the strong tradition of excursions and tours by the Colwill's family business, a proportion of the Colwills (Ilfracombe) Ltd fleet comprised charabancs. This 23-seater, No 6 (FM 1459), was one of four Daimlers with Metcalfe bodywork, again sent down from Chester in the dove-grey livery used by Crosville. *Alan Lambert collection*

the purchase of the Hardy Central Garage Co Ltd, of Minehead, Somerset. That which is pertinent to the Southern National story is the larger portion of the Hardy business, stretching westward from Lynton, on the Bristol Channel coast of North Devon, down to Newquay, on the Atlantic coast of North Cornwall. Since the Hardy fleet in the section had operated as the 'Hardy-Colwills Motor Bus Service', some explanation is necessary.

The 'Colwill' part of the fleetname had been retained by James Hardy to keep alive the considerable cachet attached thereto in the area around Ilfracombe — the largest seaside resort on the North Devon coast. Sam Colwill's Posting Establishment had from 1875 built up a reputation for a highly efficient 'coach and four' service to Lynton and for excursions elsewhere. His son, Tom, having died after Sam retired, Sam's daughter, Laura Colwill, determined to keep the business going and became 'motorised' in the modern manner. In 1918 Laura conferred with recently retired Army captain Geoffrey Cecil Shiers, of Rockland, Ilfracombe. He, the owner of two motor charabancs, agreed to pool his resources mechanical with those of Colwill. At the height of the 1919 season Claude Crosland Taylor, of Crosville Motor Co Ltd (not 'Services' until much later) of Crane Wharf, Chester, took a holiday in the resort and met both Shiers and Colwill. Clearly charmed, Taylor took the decision to risk floating a completely detached operation in faraway Devon.

Colwills (Ilfracombe) Ltd was registered on 21 February 1920. Its directors were Claude Crosland Taylor (Chairman), Capt Shiers and Henry Hill Coleridge, also of Ilfracombe. Additional subscribers were John Goodban, George C. Taylor, Winthrop ('Jim') C. Taylor and James Armstrong, an Ilfracombe gas engineer. Laura Colwill took 500 shares in the new company, which had a nominal capital of £25,000.

By 31 March 1921 the Crosville Motor Co had itself invested £12,757 in Colwills (Ilfracombe) Ltd.

A fleet of 18 saloon buses and charabancs, largely registered in Chester, whence they were supplied, was at work by the summer of 1922. Vehicles of Daimler, Leyland and Crossley manufacture ran daily services from Ilfracombe or Barnstaple to Bude, Combe Martin, Croyde, Georgeham, Lee Bay, Westward Ho! and Woolacombe, together with a continuing in-season coach trade. Unfortunately, in winter the latter found absolutely no custom whatsoever. In 1922 a working agreement was arranged with the Hardy Central Garage Co Ltd to avoid competition on the Combe Martin bus route, Hardy's vehicles from Lynton meeting up at that point with Colwill's from Ilfracombe. Said *Motor Transport* (1922) excitedly: '... thus providing the necessary link to complete a chain of services right away into Cornwall' — well, as far as Bude Bay at that stage!

*Above:* A small-capacity Crossley stage-carriage vehicle was also in the Crosville-supported Colwills fleet, together with two charabancs upon identical chassis. No 16 (FM 2187) was a 19-seater used for short trips in high summer; although equipped for such work it has not been fitted with the usual acetylene lights. *Alan Lambert collection*

*Left:* Believed to be one of a pair of Devon-registered Leyland G7s originally in the Colwills fleet, this vehicle nevertheless features the open rear (covered by canvas) favoured early on by Crosville. Now in Hardy-Colwills dark red, it stands ready to go on service between Barnstaple and South Molton. *Alan Lambert collection*

*Right:* This Leyland RAF-type (with Leyland-designed bodywork) still displays its World War 1 towing hooks. Hardy-Colwills No 50 (TA 6882), in the later red and cream livery, is marked up for a journey to Westward Ho! — the journey at the time more interesting than the terminus, described in 1910 as 'a miserable, half-derelict townlet'. Charles Kingsley has much to answer for!
*Alan Lambert collection*

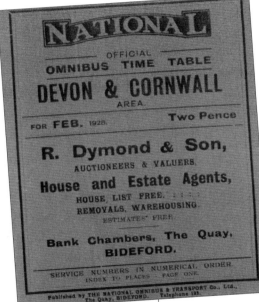

By the summer of 1922, however, Claude Crosland Taylor had decided that Devon was too far away from Cheshire to enable him to keep an eye upon things (a view he was to take also of Croscols Ltd at Tiverton, which was not a subsidiary of Colwills (Ilfracombe) Ltd — see *Glory Days: Devon General*). On 18 September Taylor discreetly withdrew, his place as a director being taken by James Hardy. Rather more careful co-ordination of services followed, and the network was extended farther south-west to Boscastle, Tintagel and Launceston. On 31 March 1924 and for a consideration of £28,340

Colwills (Ilfracombe) Ltd became the property of the Hardy Central Garage Co Ltd.

Hardy promptly located the new Hardy-Colwills headquarters at Strand, Barnstaple, and leapfrogged on to Newquay and Wadebridge with the purchases of the Newquay Motor Co Ltd and the Newquay Charabanc Co Ltd, filling in thereafter to Bodmin, Padstow and back up to Launceston. It was Hardy-Colwills which secured the lease of land at Westward Ho! from the defunct Bideford, Westward Ho! & Appledore Railway Co for use as a bus terminal upon that windswept shore. It also did the original spadework at Bideford which was to lead to that town's housing National's area headquarters and engineering works.

In February 1927 National purchased Hardy-Colwills for £48,500, which sum included Hardy's separate Minehead & District operation, destined to become part of Western National territory. The services now administered from an office at The Quay, Bideford, as 'The Devon & Cornwall Area'

*Right:* This Lancia Pentaiota has been lengthened with the aid of an additional third axle. The crew chatting at the front seem to have parked it successfully across the storm-gulley down the centre of the Strand, Barnstaple, so grounding of the stern is unlikely here, at least. The vehicle, ex Hardy-Colwills of that town, is No 2465 (UO 478), a 32-seater saloon. It was sold before the formation of Southern National.
*Eric Surfleet*

18

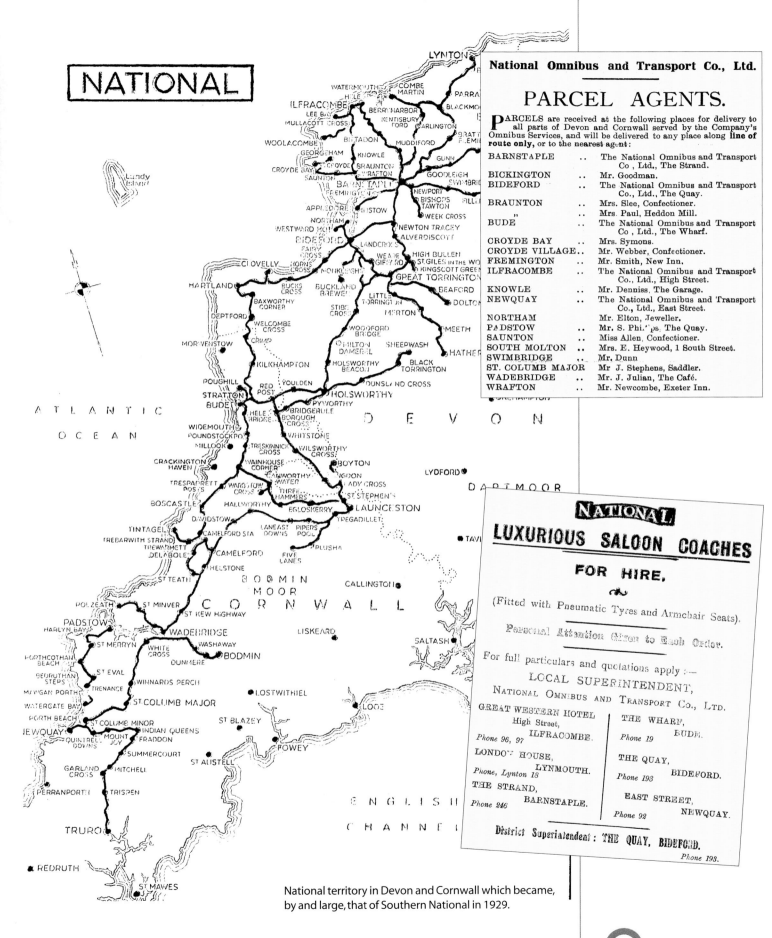

# NATIONAL

## National Omnibus and Transport Co., Ltd.

## PARCEL AGENTS.

PARCELS are received at the following places for delivery to all parts of Devon and Cornwall served by the Company's Omnibus Services, and will be delivered to any place along line of route only, or to the nearest agent:

| | |
|---|---|
| BARNSTAPLE | .. The National Omnibus and Transport Co , Ltd., The Strand. |
| BICKINGTON | .. Mr. Goodman. |
| BIDEFORD | .. The National Omnibus and Transport Co., Ltd., The Quay. |
| BRAUNTON | .. Mrs. Slee, Confectioner. |
| " | .. Mrs. Paul, Heddon Mill. |
| BUDE | .. The National Omnibus and Transport Co , Ltd., The Wharf. |
| CROYDE BAY | .. Mrs. Symons. |
| CROYDE VILLAGE | .. Mr. Webber, Confectioner. |
| FREMINGTON | .. Mr. Smith, New Inn. |
| ILFRACOMBE | .. The National Omnibus and Transport Co., Ltd., High Street. |
| KNOWLE | .. Mr. Denniss, The Garage. |
| NEWQUAY | .. The National Omnibus and Transport Co., Ltd., East Street. |
| NORTHAM | .. Mr. Elton, Jeweller. |
| PADSTOW | .. Mr. S. Phi..ps, The Quay. |
| SAUNTON | .. Miss Allen, Confectioner. |
| SOUTH MOLTON | .. Mrs. E. Heywood, 1 South Street. |
| SWIMBRIDGE | .. Mr. Dunn |
| ST. COLUMB MAJOR | Mr J. Stephens, Saddler. |
| WADEBRIDGE | .. Mr. J. Julian, The Café. |
| WRAFTON | .. Mr. Newcombe, Exeter Inn. |

## NATIONAL
## LUXURIOUS SALOON COACHES
### FOR HIRE.

(Fitted with Pneumatic Tyres and Armchair Seats).

Personal Attention Given to Each Order.

For full particulars and quotations apply :—

LOCAL SUPERINTENDENT,
NATIONAL OMNIBUS AND TRANSPORT CO., LTD.

| | |
|---|---|
| GREAT WESTERN HOTEL High Street, ILFRACOMBE. Phone 96, 97 | THE WHARF, BUDE. Phone 19 |
| LONDON HOUSE, LYNMOUTH. Phone, Lynton 18 | THE QUAY, BIDEFORD. Phone 193. |
| THE STRAND, BARNSTAPLE. Phone 246 | EAST STREET, NEWQUAY. Phone 92. |

District Superintendent: THE QUAY, BIDEFORD.
Phone 193.

National territory in Devon and Cornwall which became, by and large, that of Southern National in 1929.

# Tilling's and SR's Southern National

As the 1920s were drawing to a close two major pieces of legislation came to fruition in Parliament — legislation which would have a profound influence upon the road passenger-transport industry in the United Kingdom. The first would concern the major territorial bus companies, the second virtually everyone in the business, right down to the local country-bus owner who plied his trade with but one vehicle.

The origins of the first may be traced to varying degrees of activity in the West Country — in locations which would eventually become the territories of Southern National or Western National, namely the involvement of railway companies in the provision of motor buses as less costly extensions to their existing railway lines. It is generally accepted that the absolute pioneer was Sir George Newnes, who, as Chairman of the narrow-gauge Lynton & Barnstaple Railway, in May 1903 put into service two Milnes-Daimler 16hp 22-seater wagonettes to connect with Ilfracombe from the L&B's Blackmoor station. In a corner of England which was one of the last to give up regular horse-drawn road transport, their appearance caused much use of lavender nosegays. Bystanding ladies didn't like them either. The Devon Constabulary was called in and, with stopwatches and handkerchief signalling, deduced that one of the drivers had exceeded the 8mph speed limit. Sir George was appalled at such ingratitude and withdrew the service that July.

The beneficiary of this response was the Great Western Railway, which snapped up both vehicles and put them into service where the local folk were made of much sterner stuff — in Cornwall. On 17 August 1903 the GWR began running between Helston railway station and The Lizard. This proved to be the kick-start for over 30 years' motor-bus operation by the GWR, with by far the largest fleet owned by a railway company. The London & South Western — forerunner of the Southern Railway — nevertheless beat the GWR by a short head in June 1904 to become the first to serve Chagford, Devon, with a route from Queen Street station in Exeter (see *Glory Days: Devon General*).

Two decades later those railway companies actually running motor omnibuses were advised that it would be wise if such activities were properly regularised by legislation. The four main-line British railway companies gained the appropriate powers when four separate Railway (Road Transport) Acts became law on 3 August 1928. Once such powers had been granted, however, each sought instead to buy its way into the established territorial motor-bus industry. The railway companies were to claim their stakeholdings in bus-operating firms on the grounds of geographical contiguity, in order, primarily, that appropriate road/rail connections could be developed. In most cases this meant purchasing a one-third holding in each territorial company, equal to the shares held by the Tilling & British Automobile Traction Co Ltd (the other third being held by independent investors). In the case of National, not party to a T&BAT arrangement, a 50:50 division of ownership offered itself as the way forward.

All four main-line railway companies ran through one or other of the separated territories of the National Omnibus & Transport Co Ltd. In Essex, Bedfordshire and Hertfordshire the London, Midland & Scottish and the London & North Eastern railway companies agreed in principle to pool their interests. In the West Country the GWR, which had a large part of its motor-bus fleet already based there, preferred separate consideration — an option agreed to by the Southern Railway, particularly in the light of the traditional rivalry between its LSWR forebear and the Great Western, still extant under its original name.

The National Omnibus & Transport Co Ltd (No 114932) was to become by and large a holding company. The operating area in which the GWR was to take a half share got off the ground first as the Western National Omnibus Co Ltd (No 236066).

Great Western Road Motor No 1 sets off from Helston railway station for the Lizard on 17 August 1903, in the days before registration numbers. The vehicle, one of a pair, was a 16hp Milnes-Daimler 22-seater. The two vehicles were second-hand by a few weeks only, having worked briefly for the Ilfracombe Motor Coach Co; thereafter they set in motion the large GWR Road Motor Department, which was to play an important part in National's history. *Alan Lambert collection*

As early as December 1929 Southern National began to cast covetous eyes upon the excursions-and-tours business of W. Pennell King, which National had agreed he should keep when he agreed to withdraw his Crewkerne–Yeovil stage-carriage service in 1923. It was decided that 'a hint' should be broadcast, courtesy of the Southern Railway, about possible competition 'which might have the effect of drawing from Mr King that he would consider the disposal of his coach business'. That didn't work. Pennell King relied upon the terms of the 1923 agreement. In April 1930 Southern National was advised (by counsel's opinion) that 'the agreement entered into by National is equally binding upon the company'. It was agreed instead that lawyers be instructed to approach Mr King without disclosing that they were interested on behalf of this company' (did it really believe he wouldn't guess?) and find out whether his business was for sale — and, if so, at what price.

The lengthy acquisitional charade continued. Pennell King was not prepared to accept less than £4,000. The company dangled the bait of a Crewkerne agency agreement before him. By December the empty line was reeled in, for at one stage he offered his business for £7,000 including his garage in Lyme Road — or £6,000 without it. Quite apart from the travel facilities he provided for the people of Crewkerne and district for a decade with his own vehicles, he deserves to be recorded as one of the most shrewd negotiators Southern National encountered. The deal was finally settled in February 1932: Pennell King sold his coaching business for £4,250, plus solicitor's charges, together with five medium-sized coaches — three Reos, a Commer and a Bedford. He then became an agent for Southern National in Crewkerne and ran a distinguished local car dealership.

Meanwhile, in April 1930, Southern National acquired the lease of covered accommodation with which to enhance its Bridport depot. It also purchased the business of Frank Squire of Barnstaple — £150 for his goodwill and £350 for his 19-seat Guy coach — and bought a 16-seat Chevrolet bus from A. Braund, of Braunton, near Barnstaple, for £324 7s 2d (£324.36). An offer of sale from W. H. Robins, also of Barnstaple, was declined.

In January 1930 Hants & Dorset Motor Services Ltd had been approached with a view to a joint service between Weymouth and Bournemouth. Hants & Dorset was at that time caught up in a battle with the 10 buses of Poole & District Motor Services Ltd and made the surprising suggestion (even allowing for the 'poker-playing' wiles of H&D's William Wells Graham) that it should be run entirely by Southern National, which, in turn,

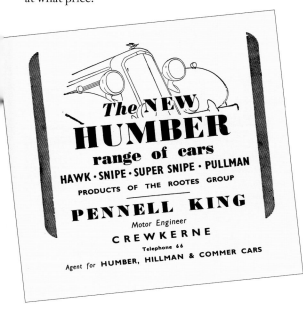

The NEW **HUMBER**
range of cars
HAWK · SNIPE · SUPER SNIPE · PULLMAN
PRODUCTS OF THE ROOTES GROUP

**PENNELL KING**
Motor Engineer
CREWKERNE
Telephone 66
Agent for HUMBER, HILLMAN & COMMER CARS

promptly suspected that 'difficulties might arise with regard to licensing at Bournemouth'. Following what turned out to be 'a very friendly meeting' in June between Bert Smith and W. W. Graham, principally to discuss a joint takeover of George Vacher's Bere Regis Motor Service (an arrangement whereby Hants & Dorset would actually gain some territory to the west of a previously agreed demarcation line), Hants & Dorset seems to have been reassured of Southern National's basically amicable intent. The joint Weymouth–Bournemouth service started on Saturday 26 July 1930 and was extended to Southwell (Portland) in December, Hants & Dorset withdrawing north to Weymouth only from 1 January 1931. In Bert Smith, incidentally, the National companies enjoyed the services of a great asset. Throughout the previous decade, for instance, he had developed a good working relationship with Devon General's Daniel Campbell.

The co-ordination of road and rail facilities received early attention compared with most other territorial companies outside the South West. A local committee was set up which comprised Lambert and Buszard (SN) and McBright and Short (SR). Four months later (July 1930) 27 ordinary and period excursions had been set up as follows: Appledore via Bideford station; Beaminster via Crewkerne station; Bedruthan Steps via Padstow station; Bovington Camp via Wool station; Camelford (Masons Arms) via Camelford station; Charminster via Dorchester station; Charmouth via Lyme Regis station; Chickerell via Weymouth station; Combe Martin via Ilfracombe station; Hartland via Bideford station; Kingston via Corfe Castle station; Lulworth Cove via Wool station; Lynton via Barnstaple Junction; Marhamchurch via Bude station; Misterton via Crewkerne station; Mosterton via Crewkerne station; Newquay via Wadebridge station; Northam via Bideford station;

St Columb Major via Wadebridge station; Saunton via Braunton station; Shaftesbury via Gillingham (Dorset) station; Stratton via Bude station; Trevone via Padstow station; Uplyme via Axminster station; Westward Ho! via Bideford station; Widemouth Bay via Bude station; and Zeals via Gillingham (Dorset) station. These were followed by five rail and road tours centred upon Ilfracombe and by inter-availability arrangements for 11 locations in the Somerset & Dorset area. The period of availability of road and rail combined tickets coincided with that of the rail portions of the tickets.

Several other concessions toward Southern Railway interests took the form of the cartage of goods train traffic in specially adapted vehicles from Camelford station to Boscastle and to romantic Tintagel. In addition, reciprocal arrangements were set up in the event of vehicular breakdown or the blockage of railway lines — the passengers to be transferred, where possible, to the other mode of transport. Ilfracombe depot supplied petrol for SR goods lorries in that area, and elsewhere running repairs were carried out at Southern National depots.

The second piece of legislation, which, in the main, benefited the major territorial companies, was the Road Traffic Act 1930. The country was divided into 'Traffic Areas', each with a Traffic Commissioner empowered to preside over 'traffic courts' and decide the routes to be followed, the timetables to be adhered to and (most importantly), in the face of objection from competitors, existent or potential, which operator should be granted the necessary licences. Initially several Southern National services started their journeys in one traffic area and terminated in another, so that one starting in the Western Area required a 'backing licence' from the Southern Area commissioners and *vice versa*, until after a few years it was decided to dispense with the latter area — which tidied things up considerably.

In 1931, after lengthy and somewhat complicated negotiations with W. Mumford of Plymouth, Western National took over the fleet and services of his Southern General Omnibus Co. One vehicle still 'in the pipeline' was this Reo FB 16-seater, which Mumford completed for Southern National. It became No 3112 (DR 8729).
*Eric Surfleet*

In February 1931 Thomas Tilling Ltd, through the good offices of its subsidiary, Tilling Motor Services, purchased a controlling interest in the National Omnibus & Transport Co Ltd, paying £2 3s 0d (£2.15) per £1 share. First of the NO&T directors to leave the board were Col the Hon Stuart Pleydell-Bouverie and Henry Merrett. They were replaced with effect from May 1931 by Tilling's George Cardwell. One year later Bert Smith resigned his directorship. His 100 6% preference shares were transferred to Tilling's formidable John Frederick Heaton, who took his place on the board and was thereafter elevated to Chairman of both companies. Tilling's Percival Stone Clark was brought in as general manager and David Tuff as 'Assistant Engineer'. In November 1932, Sir John Jarvis Bt and Walter J. Iden resigned as directors, to be replaced by Tilling's Stanley Kennedy and quickly-promoted Stone Clark. The registered office of SN/WN was transferred forthwith to Exeter.

The position of the Southern Railway representatives of course remained unchanged, but Gilbert Szlumper, probably reading the runes aright, made much of the 'difficulties in the way' of any attempt to amalgamate Southern National with Western National.

This was the time of the Great Depression. That, plus a couple of summer seasons which had suffered appalling weather conditions had brought poor receipts to large and small operators alike. The larger firms were, of course, better placed to survive this, and in 1932 the after-effects of the Road Traffic Act 1930 gathered momentum. Over a 12-month period the following operators sold out to Southern National: Wincanton Motor Services (£1,000),

Thomas H. Bassett, Braunton (£400), Mrs E. Ellwood, Bradford Abbas (£50), Hockin & Co, Sutcombe, Holsworthy (£400), B. C. Toogood ('Peter Pan'), Shaftesbury (£300), Waldon Bros, Ilfracombe (£250), Copps & Autocars (Ilfracombe) Ltd, (£2,000), George 'Charlie' Brend, Bideford (£1,000), S. Lang, Bideford (£600), William J. Ashton, Parkham, Bideford (£180), Mrs B. M. Ley, Parkham, Bideford (£180), Edwards & Hann Ltd, Beaminster (£1,500) and Chaplin & Rogers (Chard Motors), a joint purchase with Western National (£4,500, of which £2,581 was paid by Southern National).

Following the formation of the separate National 'regional' companies W. J. Iden had taken a keen interest in whether or not each should have a separate fleet colour scheme — and had gone to the trouble of having the directors look at three specially painted examples. Now that he'd gone, on 18 January 1933 Tilling made its momentous æsthetic decision: 'green is to be continued as the colour of Southern National buses'. Tilling also reviewed the cost of delivering new vehicles by rail — and decided to collect them by road instead.

By way of making a reciprocal mark, the board's SR representatives took a firm stance when Western National bought the business of Dunn's Services of Taunton in May 1933. Two of the 11 services involved went beyond Honiton to reach the South Coast at Sidmouth and Seaton. The former was in Devon General's area, but the latter was very much SN territory — yet WN was not inclined to agree that SN should participate. A paper-war ensued, and it was not until a year later that, upon payment of £250, Southern National won the day. *Vive la différence!*

Two Thornycroft BC chassis had also been ordered by Mumford at the time of Western National's acquisition of Southern General. W. Mumford Ltd of Billacombe built the 26-seat bodywork for the pair, which entered service instead with Southern National. DR 8728 became No 3108 in the Southern National fleet. *Colin Morris collection*

*Above:* This vehicle was the first of many bodied for both Southern and Western National by Eastern Counties of Lowestoft. A 32-seater, No 66 (OD 7778) was a TSM B39A7 delivered in 1934, after this photograph was taken for the bodybuilder, whose trademark appears in front of the operator's address block. TSM's low-line engine and radiator were unusual for the time. *Calton Phoenix*

*Top right:* Delivered to Edwards & Hann Ltd in 1929 through the good offices of S. H. Vincent of Yeovil was this Thornycroft A6 with 24-seat 'Emerald' bodywork built by Challands Ross. It was registered TK 4474 and operated between Beaminster and Bridport. When Southern National purchased the business in 1933 this vehicle entered the fleet as No 3430.
*Colin Morris collection*

*Upper and lower left:* During 1933 Southern National took delivery of 16 TSM B39A7 saloons with 35-seat bodywork by Brush of Loughborough, the chassis costing £356 10s 0d each, the wooden-framed bodies £360 each. The chassis, if not the original engines and bodywork, were destined to last much longer than expected. This was No 54 (FJ 8973) when new, the interior view showing the seat moquette of the period.
*Colin Morris collection*

On 7 March 1935 the share capital of the Southern National Omnibus Co Ltd was increased from £500,000 to £550,000, most of which was taken up by the National Omnibus & Transport Co Ltd. At the same time, it was agreed that NO&T should continue to hold the lease on the 206 Brompton Road premises on behalf of its subsidiary companies. Meanwhile SN had purchased the two local services and four saloon buses of Dorchester Motor Services, together with some property, for

*Right:* By virtue of both having railway lines into Weymouth the Great Western and Southern railways operated a joint bus service between Radipole, Weymouth and Wyke Regis. A GWR/SR Maudslay ML3 saloon poses in front of the Southern National garage — ex Road Motors — at Dorchester Road, Radipole. Southern National took over the service (after a fashion — see text) from 1 January 1934.
*Alan Lambert collection*

*Lower right:* From 1935 the dark-green bands of the National Omnibus & Transport era were replaced by cream. This, together with a gold line beneath the waistrail, gave the fleet a brighter image, similar to that of Southdown. Even the 'old stagers' received the same treatment, as this unidentified 1929 Leyland Titan TD1, in original form, demonstrates at Bude in 1938.
*Alan Lambert collection*

£2,000. At Barnstaple, for £4,250, it had bought a site at Boutport Street upon which a garage would later be built for some £10,000. Also at this time a garage was acquired for £4,073 in Station Road, Seaton. A further £2,250 was being spent upon the rebuilding of Chard garage, and the Yeovil premises were earmarked for a facelift.

The latter half of the 1930s saw the national economy emerge gradually but surely out from the economic depression. Since car ownership was

*Right and below:* Already equipped to work for Southern National in its Somerset & Dorset area, a brand-new Dennis Ace of 1935 is pictured at the Brush Electrical Engineering Co's coachworks at Loughborough. This sporty little 20-seater, No 760 (ATT 182), was among the last vehicles to enter service with dark-green waistline and this style of fleetname. *Colin Morris collection*

not yet commonplace the bus and coach industry's finances began to improve, noticeably so on services in — and to — the beautiful West Country. Acquisitions of smaller competitors continued apace, but in many instances rather more vendors now sold up in order to retire in relative financial comfort. A rough guide to the increased sums of money available to a Southern National firmly backed by Tilling is provided by the following examples of acquisitions made during the run-up toward World War 2 (which event put the tin hat upon such things): A. F. Baker ('Pride of Lyme'), Lyme Regis (£1,400), Greyhound Coaches (Weymouth) Ltd, including 13 coaches and a garage at Chickerell (£25,000), A. K. Hardy ('Scarlet Pimpernel'), Ilfracombe (£3,050 — of which WN paid £558 for its share of the express work), E. B. Hocking 'Ensign Carriages', Appledore (£5,500), Sully & Sons, Chard (joint purchase £21,470, of which WN paid £10,530, largely on account of its connections with Taunton), F. W. Powell ('Orange & Black Coaches'), Branscombe (£5,425), C. R. Good ('Pioneer Service'), Beer (£2,775), Portland Express group (£16,750), comprising R. J. Fancy, Easton (£7,100), F. H. Hoare, Portland (£5,000) and L. A. S. Toleman, Portland (£4,650), W. H. Charles, Leigh, Sherborne (£370), Executors of Stephen Crabb, Uploders (£100), Bird Bros (Transport) Ltd, Yeovil (£860), Lovell & Ford ('The Safety Coaches'), Corfe Castle (£1,500), Bartlett & Nichols, Langton Matravers (£2,000, plus employment for Leonard Nichols as manager of SN's depot at Swanage, which post he was to hold from 1937 to 1951), Mrs E. M. Jeanes

*Left:* Basically a forward-control version of the Ace, the Dennis Mace was able to provide six more seats, plus a luggage pen, yet still offered the comparatively small turning-circle of its forebear. No 661 (BTA 52) was one of nine 26-seat saloons with bodywork by Eastern Counties, delivered in 1935. It is seen taking a rest at Bude some three yeas later. *Alan Lambert collection*

*Above:* This Leyland Tiger TS2, with chassis and engine dating from 1929, was originally fitted with 31-seat Beadle coachwork. In 1936, however, No 2865 (UU 9416), still sporting its original radiator and enamelled tiger's-head badge, was rebodied as a 32-seat coach, principally for tours work, by W. Mumford Ltd.
*Calton Phoenix*

*Right:* In June 1936 Southern National acquired A.K. Harding's excursions, tours and express services based in Ilfracombe. His 'Scarlet Pimpernel' fleetname was considered to have sufficient cachet in the resort for the name to be retained — for some 20 years! Southern National Bedford WTB/Duple coach 3663 (AOD 870), new that year, is seen in Minehead in Scarlet Pimpernel's red and cream livery.
*W. J. Haynes / Andrew Waller collection*

*Left:* One of 11 vehicles which entered service with Southern National in April 1936 when Sully of Chard was acquired was this forward-control Leyland Cub. No 3648 (AYD 169) was one of a pair of SKP3 Cubs with 26-seat bodywork by Thurgood of Ware. It was sent far from home to Bideford, where, on 18 August 1946, it awaits a departure for Ilfracombe.
*The Omnibus Society*

*Above:* In 1936 Southern National chose to purchase six Leyland TS7D six-wheelers, following the hire for demonstration purposes of a similar vehicle owned by Southdown. The task had been to take large numbers of tourists up to Portland in safety along a road frequently threatened by strong winds. No 1002 (ETA 235) and its companions — with 44-seat bodywork by Beadle — entered service in July 1937. It is pictured in Weymouth in August 1953. *Alan B. Cross*

*Right:* One of two AEC Regals fitted with a large luggage compartment at the rear and extended roof pannier for service through the villages once served by the now-closed Lynton & Barnstaple narrow-gauge railway. Photographed at the Barnstaple end on 6 August 1952 is No 3904 (TK 6519), new in 1931. The Beadle body seen here was fitted in 1938. *Alan B. Cross*

('Gem Coaches'), Weymouth (£775), C. F. Gillham ('Blue Bird Coaches'), Bridport (£800), and Simpson & Sons, Woolacombe (£550). The 'Greyhound' name was retained by SN at Weymouth for two seasons, while the 'Scarlet Pimpernel' name and livery were held in such high regard at Ilfracombe that SN kept them in being until well after World War 2 (see Chapter 4).

During this period also title to 55-58 Queen Street, Exeter, was bought from the Southern Railway by Western National (two thirds of the price) and Southern National (one third) as their new head offices, to be followed by the purchase of 54 Queen Street as additional head-office accommodation. And on 22 April 1938 Southern National paid the grand sum of £50 to Devon General, which transferred to the company the title of its service 52 (Seaton–Beer–Sidmouth). This was part of a revised territorial agreement between the two companies, signed on 20 January 1938.

1940 Turnchapel station, the SR terminus, was totally destroyed in an air raid, whilst GWR trains coming up from or going down to Cornwall travelled by arrangement upon the Southern lines, so that they might avoid Plymouth. As Bernard Darwin (1946) wrote, 'Never before had that most lordly of Great Western trains, the Cornish Riviera Express, so far demeaned itself as to pass through comparatively humble Wadebridge … this is just one illustration of the way in which the Southern and the Great Western helped each other in difficulties …'. One more example, on 23 April 1941, saw all communications between Plymouth and Devonport cut off, and an emergency service had to be arranged with Exeter, the GWR trains running over Southern lines. Five days later, by way of tit-for-tat, Southern trains travelled over GW lines from Exeter, while GW trains were still using the SR's North Cornwall lines! In short, each company came to the rescue of the other with unfailing readiness.

To all bar the railway shareholders involved the very reason for setting up separate Southern National and Western National companies a decade or so previously now seemed somewhat less important. Earlier proposals for a merger, which had so alarmed a Gilbert Szlumper anxious to retain the historical allegiances, appeared less of a threat. But for a preoccupation with a socio-political upheaval which followed postwar, it could well have been that such 'trains of thought' might have brought about such a merger rather sooner than they eventually did.

By 1942 the problem of finding a reasonably efficient and safe method of fuelling buses with producer gas had been solved — by William Morison, now Chief Engineer at Eastern National. He had decided that the answer was to put the power unit in a trailer. The Bristol Tramways & Carriage Co Ltd agreed and mass-produced the T2 trailer for both Tilling and BET subsidiaries — and a long-suffering Leyland Titan (No 2985) from Bideford turned up with such a trailer for service at Weymouth. On 1 July 1942 Heaton was able to announce that three Southern National vehicles so fitted were in operation and were to be joined in the near future by another 16. They trundled about at several locations until in 1944 they tended to get in the way of the military rather than contribute any further to the war effort. Earlier, in the autumn of 1943, with the tide of war turning strongly in favour of Britain and her Allies, Southern National began to repurchase from the Ministry of Supply vehicles previously requisitioned, Nos 764, 772, 2608 and 3548 being among the first to return.

The first half of 1944 was a time of great upheaval in the Southern National operating areas as British, Canadian and American forces began preparing for the invasion of Normandy. Somerset and Dorset in particular became locations for the stockpiling of American military hardware and its attendant personnel. Whilst the major assault in June 1944 was launched from Southampton, Weymouth/Portland was activated as Sub-Port C on 12 November, when the Allied follow-up went into overdrive. A thoroughly unpredictable pattern

*Above:* John F. Heaton (Sir Frederick Heaton from 1942), Chairman of Southern National (and much else) 1933-1948. To quote John Hibbs (1968), 'Heaton *was* Tillings … In its obituary the *Railway Gazette* remarked:"the keynote of his success was his ability to persuade others that he could make more money for them by running their businesses than they could themselves." *Colin Morris collection*

*Left:* Originally fitted with a 32-seat Brush body, No 126 (FJ 8956) was a Bristol H originally allotted to Western National. It received this 35-seat Bristol replacement body in 1942. The vehicle has paused in Barnstaple on local service 112, which ran between Bishops Taunton and Bradiford — a journey of some three miles. *M. P. Rowledge / Ian Allan Library*

*Left:* Pictured in Taunton during World War 2, former Silver Cars coach DV 1072 now has a 32-seat Bristol saloon bus body, fitted in 1937. As part of a wartime fuel-economy measure this Leyland Tiger was, by July 1942, one of 19 Southern National vehicles already fitted with Bristol-built T2 type gas trailer. They burned specially treated anthracite — and were designed by National's William Morison. *The Omnibus Society*

*Right:* During the second half of World War 2 double-deckers also towed Bristol T-type gas trailers, as did some downgraded Royal Blue coaches. Leyland Titan TD1 No 2907 (DR 5198) of 1929 — by now a Bideford-based vehicle (see page 22) — has come to rest beside a stone-and-concrete-built (and hopefully blast-proof) surface air-raid shelter. *The Omnibus Society*

*Left:* Taunton and Chard were both depots capable of stoking up and maintaining the Bristol-built T2-type gas trailer. An example is attached to No 184 (ATT 934), a Bristol JJW/Beadle Royal Blue coach pressed into service from 1942 onward disguised as a Southern National service bus. *The Omnibus Society*

of passenger loadings in the Weymouth area was just one more problem with which the staff of this sorely tried depot of Southern National had to deal.

During World War 2 the Ministry of War Transport authorised a total sanction of just eight double-deck vehicles for Southern National — Nos 357-9 (Bristol K5G/ECW 56-seaters) 360 (K5G/Duple 55-seater), 80 (Guy Arab/Strachans 55-seater) and 361-3 (K6A/Strachans 55-seaters). The company also received 10 Bedford OWB/Duple saloons (Nos 505-14). All save 357-9 were fitted with bodywork designed and built to the spartan utility pattern of the period. The fact that these 18 vehicles represented the entire new-bus intake between 1941 and the close of 1944 gives an indication of the 'make-do and-mend' policy that the company was obliged to adopt at a time when private motoring was virtually banned.

The problem of dealing with resultant passenger demand was partially eased by a Government Order permitting the rearrangement of the seating on some saloon buses whereby, save those at the rear, all were set in two facing rows down each side of the interior. This created a large 'strap-hanging' standing area for up to 28 additional passengers — and such saloons based at Bideford and Weymouth staggered along with some difficulty on hilly sections of route. Through such swaying masses of humanity struggled fare-collecting conductresses. What was there to hang on to as they carried out the task? A ticket rack proved a useful defence against the more amorously inclined standees.

In July 1944 and in confident anticipation of a successful outcome to the war, there commenced a complicated but fascinating programme of refurbishment. No 53 (FJ 8971), a 1933-vintage

*Right:* The weather doesn't look too good as an intrepid gathering of outward-bounders have a last-minute discussion before joining their colleagues aboard a classic example of a World War 2 bus. No 511 (DOD 560) was one of seven Bedford OWB saloons delivered to Southern National in 1943 with Duple 32-seat bodywork at its most austere.
*The Omnibus Society*

*Below:* Photographed in Bideford at the conclusion of World War 2 — but still dressed in overall grey — is a rather tired-looking No 68 (OD 7780). A TSM B39A7 of 1934, one of a batch of 11 for Southern National, it still bears its original 32-seat Eastern Counties saloon body. The choice of bodybuilder represented a further step into the Tilling empire.
*The Omnibus Society*

Tilling-Stevens (or, more properly by this time, TSM) B39A7, became the first of 14 saloons of this type to have its original Brush body replaced by Eastern Coach Works in suitably relaxed utility-inspired style. This followed the fitting of a four-cylinder Gardner diesel engine and the replacement of its TSM front axle and radiator by items of Bristol manufacture. The result was a clean-lined but heavily disguised vehicle fit to match the 'New Look' fashion statement about to become popular among young ladies postwar. ECW finished its part of such work in March 1946 — one month after just one other of that batch (No 58) had been completed in similar Tilling style by Beadle at Dartford.

In deference to Western National's large loss of vehicles at Plymouth, plus its need to provide adequate transport in and out of that devastated city, only three of 16 Leyland Tiger saloons purchased second-hand from Eastern Counties (now firmly in the Tilling camp) were allocated to Southern National. When, soon afterwards, Western National received four Leyland Lion saloons from the same source, Southern National was granted three.

Throughout the latter part of the war Eastern Coach Works had been engaged in refurbishing Leyland Titan double-deckers, usually upon their original six-bay frames, but had gone on to develop a utilitarian five-bay double-deck body used to rebody completely other Titans — usually with what was considered a 'more modern', longer Covrad radiator. Thus emerged prototypes for what became the standard Tilling postwar double-decker, the 'engineer's bus' — a Bristol K chassis fitted with a lowered and tapered PV2-type radiator and lowbridge Eastern Coach Works bodywork to seat 55. Southern National received five in 1946,

*Above:* A fascinating line-up of Southern National vehicles inside the Marlborough Road, Ilfracombe, garage at the close of World War 2. From left to right are No 668 (BTA 59) a Dennis Mace/Eastern Counties; No 3652 (YD 9534), Dennis Ace, No 2868 (UU 7664), Leyland Tiger TS2/Duple, and No 2990 (GJ 9036), AEC Regal/Duple. *Calton Phoenix*

*Left:* A remarkable trio of Southern National double-deckers lined up at Barnstaple railway station on 27 August 1946 — at left the new generation in the form of Bristol K5G/ECW No 364 (HTT 992), in the centre Southern National's only Guy Arab (and Strachans-bodied too), No 80 (GTA 833), and at right AEC Regent No 2905 (TK 3024), new in 1929 but rebodied by Beadle in 1943. Whilst the ladies chat, the little girl seems to be a bus enthusiast. *The Omnibus Society*

each fitted with a five-cylinder Gardner engine — not entirely suited to the hillier parts of the company's West Country terrain.

The Southern National company also celebrated that first year of postwar travel with the purchase of a very early example of Beadle's more remarkable offerings — a lightweight bus of integral chassisless construction using parts salvaged from retired vehicles or, in later examples, new power units from well-known manufacturers. Southern National's August 1946 *débutante* was No 2000 (FUO 481), its fleet number chosen to emphasise the new era. It was fitted with a four-cylinder diesel engine previously implanted in a Dennis saloon (the one broken by the Luftwaffe at Houndstone Camp) and the running gear from a Leyland Cub — another vehicle previously in the employ of the company. Costing a mere £1,000, it was allocated initially to

Yeovil, whence it achieved some notably economic performances.

No 2000 also cut something of a dash in the area when it first appeared on local services. I recall it pausing outside the Swan Inn at Haselbury Plucknett *en route* to Crewkerne, as a handful of regulars emerged with pints of cider — and one with a 'squeeze-box' — to serenade this 'ultra-modern' bus upon its westward way, much to the amusement of those on board. It certainly presented a remarkable but rather unfair contrast with the two-tone-red and cream Bedford OWB utility of Gunn's 'Safeway Services' of South Petherton, which, by mutual consent at that time, worked alternate journeys along that stretch of road. In a time of continuing food and clothes rationing — and general austerity — it was a symbol of a new design-conscious era ahead.

*Above:* Fitted with a new 52-seat Beadle body in 1946, Leyland TD1 Titan No 2908 (DR 5199) — at that time also sporting a gutsy six-cylinder engine — takes a rest on a parking lot carved out of a hillside. That, and the corrugated-iron barn, which invited folk to 'Queue here for Hartland and Bude', constituted Southern National's Clovelly outstation. *The Omnibus Society*

*Above right:* Behind Leyland Titan TD1 No 2854 (DR 5163), still wearing its 'pre-Tilling edict' livery upon its 1946 Beadle bodywork, comes the full-faced symbol of postwar fashion. Built with running units supplied by Southern National and delivered in 1946, chassisless No 2000 (FUO 461) was Beadle's revolutionary saloon-bus offering to the bus industry. The destination display was still in prototype form. *Alan B. Cross*

*Below:* Pictured on a short working of North Devon's flagship route 101 is No 3102 (DR 8803), a Leyland Titan TD1 delivered in 1931 with Strachans bodywork but rebodied in 1946 with this classic example of a 52-seat lowbridge design by Beadle. A six-cylinder Gardner engine fitted earlier has caused the radiator to protrude somewhat. *Calton Phoenix*

When it entered service in 1935 Bristol JJW No 188 (ATT 938) was a dashing Weymann-bodied Royal Blue coach. Always nominally a Southern National vehicle, it received a 36-seat Beadle bus body in 1948. In this latter guise it awaits passengers at Sidmouth on service 45 to Lyme Regis — in the company of a Devon General AEC Regal bound for Exeter. *D. J. Outred/Ian Allan Library*

Photographed in BTC days but very much a product of the Heaton era, No 311 (DDV 38), a Bristol L5G saloon dating from 1939, originally carried a Mumford 31-seat body. By the time this picture was taken it was a Beadle-bodied 36-seater, on service between Wincanton and Shaftesbury — a detached 'three-county' route. *The Omnibus Society*

When Tilling issued its 1947 directive that most of its subsidiaries' double-deckers should have just two cream bands several SN/WN vehicles acquired a 'slipped-down' version of what was required. This Leyland Titan TD1 of 1929, rebodied by Beadle in 1947, was one such example, still in Bude's active stable on 6 August 1952. *Alan B. Cross*

## Timetable page 31

| 7 | H 412 | |
| 7A | H 413 | |
| 7B | H 414 | |

**YEOVIL— CREWKERNE—HINTON ST. GEORGE YEOVIL—CREWKERNE. YEOVIL— CREWKERNE—SOUTH PETHERTON.** — **7 / 7A / 7B**

Including journeys operated between Yeovil—West Coker on Service No. 2, Yeovil—West Coker.

**Weekdays.**

Stops (reading down):
Yeovil (Pen Mill Station), Town Station Road, Triangle, Yeovil (Boro'), Yeovil (Hendford, Butchers Arms), West Coker (New Inn), East Chinnock (Portman Arms), Haselbury (White Horse), North Perrott (Manor Arms), Misterton (Globe Inn), Crewkerne (Station Approach), Crewkerne (Square) arr, Crewkerne (Square) dep, Merriott (Church Street), Hinton St. George, Lopen (P.O.), South Petherton.

*n.th.—Not Thursdays.   s.o.—Saturdays only.   n.s.—Not Saturdays.*

31

## Timetable page (right)

| 63 | H 4412 | SHAFTESBURY—WEST STOUR | 63 |

**Saturdays only.**

| | | | | | | | |
|---|---|---|---|---|---|---|---|
| Shaftesbury | dep | 9 15 | 1230 | 5 0 | West Stour | dep | 9 45 1 25 5 45 |
| Stour Row | ,, | 9 27 | 1245 | 5 15 | East Stour | ,, | 9 49 1 29 5 49 |
| Todber | ,, | 9 32 | 1250 | 5 20 | Stour Provost | ,, | 9 54 1 34 5 54 |
| Stour Provost | ,, | 9 35 | 1255 | 5 25 | Todber | ,, | 9 59 1 39 5 59 |
| East Stour | ,, | | | | Stour Row | ,, | |
| West Stour | arr | 9 44 | 1 0 | 5 34 | Shaftesbury | arr | 10 41 4 46 4 |

| 64 | H 4414 | YEOVIL—STALBRIDGE—SHAFTESBURY | 64 |

**Thursdays and Saturdays only.**

| | | | | | | | | s o | n s |
|---|---|---|---|---|---|---|---|---|---|
| Yeovil (Red Lion) | dep | 1015 2 15 6 15 | | | Shaftesbury | dep | 1030 | 2 30 2 30 | 6 30 |
| Sherborne (Cheap St.) | ,, | 1035 2 35 6 35 | | | East Stour | ,, | 1043 | 2 43 2 43 | 6 43 |
| Milborne Port | ,, | 1047 2 47 6 47 | | | Todber | ,, | 1050 | 2 50 2 50 | 6 50 |
| Henstridge | ,, | 1057 2 57 6 57 | | | Marnhull | ,, | 1054 | 2 54 2 54 | 6 54 |
| Stalbridge | arr | 11 23 2 7 2 | | | North Lodge | ,, | 11 53 | 3 5 | 7 5 |
| Stalbridge | dep | 1113 3 17 7 12 | | | Stalbridge | arr | 11 53 | 5 3 | 5 7 5 |
| North Lodge | ,, | 1117 3 10 3 10 7 10 | | | Stalbridge | dep | 1110 3 10 3 40 7 10 |
| Marnhull | ,, | 1128 3 28 7 28 | | | Henstridge | ,, | 1115 3 15 3 45 7 15 |
| Todber | ,, | 1132 3 32 7 32 | | | Milborne Port | ,, | 1125 3 25 3 55 7 25 |
| East Stour | ,, | 1139 3 39 7 39 | | | Sherborne (C.S.) | ,, | 1136 3 36 4 6 7 36 |
| Shaftesbury | arr | 1152 3 52 7 52 | | | Yeovil (Red L.) | arr | 1155 3 55 4 25 7 55 |

For schedule showing all journeys between Yeovil, Sherborne and Stalbridge see pages 35, 36
s.o.—Saturdays only.   n.s.—Not Saturdays.

| 83 | H 1982 | YEOVIL—EAST COKER—CORSCOMBE | 83 |

| | | Mondays | Wednesdays | Fridays |
|---|---|---|---|---|
| Yeovil (Butchers Arms) | dep | 9 55 3 30 1230 2 0 | 4 0 5 0 | 9 40 10 0 12 0 1 55 3 25 |
| Quicksilver Mail Hotel | ,, | 10 0 3 35 1235 2 5 | 4 5 5 5 | 9 55 1015 1215 2 0 3 30 |
| East Coker | ,, | 10 3 45 1245 2 15 | 4 15 5 15 | |
| Sutton Bingham | ,, | 10 20 3 55 1255 | 5 25 | 1025 |
| Halstock | ,, | | 5 25 | 1025 |
| Corscombe | arr | 1040 4 15 1 15 | 5 45 | 1045 4 10 |

| Corscombe | dep | 4 20 1 15 | | 1045 |
| Halstock | ,, | 1050 4 30 1 35 | | 1055 4 20 |
| Sutton Bingham | ,, | 11 0 4 40 1 35 | | 4 20 |
| East Coker | ,, | 1110 4 45 1 45 2 15 2 154 15 5 45 | 1115 1115 1225 2 10 4 40 |
| Quicksilver Mail Hotel | ,, | 11 20 5 0 1 55 2 25 4 25 5 55 | 1010 1130 1230 2 25 4 55 |
| Yeovil (Butchers Arms) | arr | 1125 5 5 2 0 2 30 4 30 6 0 | |

**Saturdays.**

| Yeovil (Butchers Arms) | dep | 1 30 | 4 15 | |
| Quicksilver Mail Hotel | ,, | | | |

# FOR YOUR PLEASURE . .

## "SOUTHERN NATIONAL"
# LUXURY COACH TOURS

are operated during the summer months from

| | |
|---|---|
| APPLEDORE | DORCHESTER |
| BARNSTAPLE | ILFRACOMBE |
| BEER | ILMINSTER |
| BIDEFORD | LYME REGIS |
| BRIDPORT | LYNTON |
| BRANSCOMBE | OSMINGTON |
| BRAUNTON | PADSTOW |
| BUDE | PORTLAND |
| CHARD | SEATON |
| COMBE ST. NICHOLAS | SWANAGE |
| CREWKERNE | WEYMOUTH |
| CROYDE BAY | WESTWARD HO ! |
| | YEOVIL |

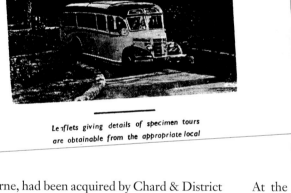

Leaflets giving details of specimen tours
are obtainable from the appropriate local

*Above:* Close-up! Keeping clean and tidy in the garage ready for a trip to the Royal Cornwall Show, and suitably displaying 'Lands End & Penzance', is Bedford OB No 1448 (LTA 924), one of 15 of the type delivered to Southern National in 1950. Coachwork was by Duple. *DWR Picture Library*

Crewkerne, had been acquired by Chard & District Coaches Ltd of Bristol. Less than a year later that firm sold its Greyhound Bus Ltd's Bridport services to Southern National, which from 14 January 1952 ran them as one between Bridport station and West Bay. With effect from 6 April 1952 Southern National bought a considerably larger operation, Blake's Bus Service Ltd, centred upon Delabole, Cornwall. Seventeen stage-carriage services (SN routes 400-416) reached out to locations as far afield as Plymouth, Bodmin and Tremore, Wadebridge, Tintagel, Boscastle, Marshgate and Launceston; also included were Blakes' local excursions and tours. Seven coaches — of Commer, Maudslay and TSM manufacture — joined the SN fleet (as 3803-9) together with eight Bedfords acting as service buses (3810-7). The purchase price, which included goodwill, premises and vehicles, was £27,500.

Between November 1952 and June 1953 Long Range Setright ticket machines at last replaced the dear old 'ker-ching' Bell Punches together with their mousetraps loaded with green and white tickets.

At the height of the summer season of 1952 (15 August) a torrential downpour of unique proportion thundered down upon Exmoor, overwhelming the riverbeds of the East and West Lyn. The resultant flash-flood descended upon Lynmouth, carrying away substantial buildings, bridges and roadways. Of the 34 people who lost their lives, most were residents of the popular resort. A description of Southern National's quick response, particularly rescue work for shocked tourists, is given in some detail by Crawley and Simpson (1990). For well over a year afterward Lynton and Lynmouth traffic was reduced considerably, largely as a result of an understandable fear of a repetition, plus the destruction of the recognisable natural attractions.

By April 1953 the architect's original plan (a barrel-roofed concrete system) for the reconstruction of Weymouth garage had been abandoned. The nationwide freeing from control of steel supplies now meant that corrugated covering on a steel frame could suffice. In preparation for this development SN bought the site of No 10 King

*Right:* This beautiful coach entered service with Southern National in 1951, one of the last of half-cab configuration, thus marking the end of an era. Standing proudly before the Radipole, Weymouth, garage on 1 July 1965, No 1322 (LTA 901) was a Bristol LL6B with 37-seat Duple coachwork. *C. L. Caddy*

*Right:* When it first arrived it impressed some and dismayed those who liked to identify a vehicle by the characteristic shape of its radiator. Enter the 'Queen Mary' or, in some companies, 'The Brabazon' — both indicating the type's comparatively large size. Bristol LWL6B/ECW 37-seat coach No 1334 (LTA 929) entered service in 1951. *C. L. Caddy*

*Right:* The first Bristol LWL saloon in the Southern National fleet, No 1600 (LTA 935) was an LWL6B with 39-seat ECW body. The vehicle was photographed in Weymouth on 5 September 1966; whilst the route number displayed suggests a journey from the Admiralty's Underwater Weapons Establishment at Portland, the rest of the information implies otherwise. *C. L. Caddy*

Street and a large property, No 8 (total £8,500), for conversion into a district traffic office, waiting room, left-luggage, parcels and enquiry offices, plus staff rest room and canteen — with valuable accommodation left over for letting purposes.

The following year it was learned that the amount recoverable from the War Damage Commission was in the region of £29,000 — £11,000 more than originally hoped for. The lowest tender for reconstruction work was £46,473, and the contract was awarded to Bird & Cox of Weymouth, the work to commence on 1 October 1954 — 14 years after the Luftwaffe had demolished it. In order to clear the site for construction Westham coach park, Melcombe Regis station yard and a council car park were utilised for overnight and layover parking. Difficulties, including a steel-erectors' strike, eventually meant that work had to be completed around parked buses — which it was, in April 1956!

Whilst this laborious process was going on, in May 1953 the stage-carriage business of James A. Wintle was acquired; included were a stage-carriage service (Bower Hinton–Yeovil) and a contract one (Bower–Hinton–Westlands) plus six vehicles (3821-3/5-7) — four Bedford OB buses and a Guy Vixen and a Leyland Cheetah coach. For best part of that

year Southern National was negotiating for the takeover of Hutchings & Cornelius of South Petherton, including its services and 13 vehicles. SN offered £42,000 but then, for reasons not explained, withdrew. Thus the H&C fleetname survived until the firm was acquired by Veronica Gunn's Safeway Services in 1978, long after the SN company's operations had been absorbed by Western National.

At a special meeting of the board of directors on 16 December 1953 it was announced that the capital of Southern National was to be raised from £550,000 to £900,000. On the same date nominees Sir Reginald H. Wilson and Sidney B. Taylor requested that their SN shares be vested instead in the BTC's portfolio.

Staff relations became a little strained in the summer of 1954. Regular staff objected to the employment of the traditional West Country part-time staff, in spite of an agreement about such things with the union. At one stage Southern National was 60 drivers and 50 conductors short of the necessary staffing level, but the outcome was foreseeable when stoppages were, in union terms, 'unofficial'.

Nevertheless, this was a summer which saw improvements in accommodation at Yeovil and a search for more vehicle-storage room at Ilfracombe and Bude. It also provided a bit of unexpected competition from Okeridge Motor Services Ltd when that firm extended its Okehampton–Torrington service onward to Bideford. In the Somerset & Dorset area Wincanton outstation was closed, while at Ilfracombe SN's 'Scarlet Pimpernel Coaches' at last lost their red-coated identities and became part of the green-and-cream coach fleet.

On 25 November 1952 a Bristol KSW6B, delivered that same year, nears the end of its long journey from Weymouth on service 34, joint with Wilts & Dorset Motor Services since January 1949. No 1850 (LTA 993), fitted with standard ECW 55-seat lowbridge bodywork, was a regular visitor in the 1950s to Endless Street bus station in Salisbury. *P.R.Forsey*

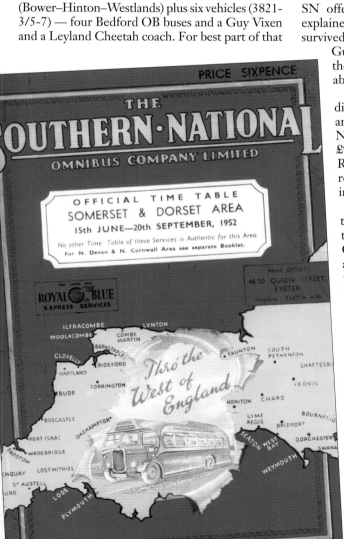

On 28 September 1957 director and General Manager Bernard Venn Smith, a workaholic, died at his desk. In appearance an 'Oliver Hardy' figure in miniature, he was remembered with respect rather than affection. He was replaced in office two months later by Thomas Gailey of the Tilling Association Ltd; he, in turn, was succeeded on 1 February 1960 by SN/WN Secretary Henry Leslie Ellis, who would still be in office as the Southern National Omnibus Company's active existence ended in 1969.

As the 1950s came toward an end unromantic railway-line closures began to lessen further the reason for a separate Southern National. SN/WN provided replacement bus services, 'few of which,' as Crawley and Simpson opined in 1990, 'turned out to be remunerative … One cannot but wonder what became of all the former rail passengers of whom not enough remained to fill a single omnibus.' Records show that this was when ladies who lived in the countryside began to purchase and drive their family's second motor car.

When, in 1959, Southern National's property in Okehampton went on the market, that pleasant town housed simply another company outstation. In contrast, after an abortive fiasco at Barnstaple, plans for a new bus station and offices at Broad Street, Ilfracombe, came to fruition in 1961, courtesy of a more thorough local-authority search team. The plan had incorporated the existing Ropery Road garage and led, in turn, to the closure of the town's Marlborough Road garage. Also in 1961 SN and WN moved across the road from their previous headquarters at 48/50 Queen Street, Exeter, into the newly completed National House at 54-58 Queen Street.

Among the service adjustments made during the 1960s was the introduction of five new works services to the new power station at Winfrith, Dorset, from points west, north and east, as well as new services to additional housing estates throughout its operating areas; the decade also saw services at Padstow, Truro and Launceston transferred to Western National, and those between Dorchester and Bere Regis to Hants & Dorset, as well as the abandonment of the Yeovil–Salisbury, Yeovil–Blandford and Yeovil–Ilminster services. The horns were being drawn in somewhat.

*Above:* What the Luftwaffe destroyed with a high-explosive bomb in October 1940 was finally restored to working order in April 1956. The Edward Street, Weymouth, garage and workshops had been put out of action; two Southern National employees had lost their lives, and 14 vehicles had been damaged. Until this new building opened the Weymouth fleet were outdoor refugees.
*John Aldridge*

## THE SOUTHERN NATIONAL
### OMNIBUS COMPANY LIMITED

Registered Offices—QUEEN STREET, EXETER.

Telephone : Exeter 4191/2/3.          Telegrams : " Natcarcom, Exeter."

### DEPOTS AND ENQUIRY OFFICES.

| Depot. | Address. | Telephone No. |
|---|---|---|
| Barnstaple | The Strand | Barnstaple 2224 |
| Bideford | The Quay | Bideford 193/4 & 641 |
| Bournemouth | { The Coach Station } { The Square } | Bournemouth 6262/3/4 |
| Bridport | South Street | Bridport 80 |
| Bude | The Strand Garage | Bude 160 |
| Chard | Cornhill | Chard 2270 |
| Delabole | Central Garage | Camelford 70 |
| Ilfracombe | High Street | Ilfracombe 96 |
| Lyme Regis | { Mr. Van H. Allen } { Broad Street } | Lyme Regis 67 |
| Lynton | Omnibus Station | Lynton 3102 |
| Newquay | 1 East Street | Newquay 2322/3 |
| Seaton | Station Road Garage | Seaton 279 |
| Weymouth | { King's Statue } { 5 Royal Terrace } | Weymouth 645/6 |
| Yeovil | { " National House " } { 67 Middle Street } | { Yeovil 1492 { Yeovil 233 |

### ENQUIRIES REGARDING THE COMPANY'S SERVICES MAY BE MADE IN LONDON AT :—

London Coastal Coaches, Ltd.,
Victoria Coach Station,
Buckingham Palace Road,
S.W. 1.
Telephone : Sloane 0202.

*Above:* The destination display on this vehicle would have raised the temperature of any passing company inspector. The vehicle itself, however, was an unusual addition to the Southern National fleet. No 375 (CVF 844) was a Bristol L5G (originally), one of six purchased from Eastern Counties in 1954 and lengthened — and one of three given 43-seat Bristol bodies. *C. L. Caddy*

*Left:* At Swanage bus station on 4 August 1957 stands No 1873 (OTT 46), Southern National's first Lodekka. A Bristol LD6B with 58-seat ECW bodywork, it was delivered in 1954. The deep radiator grille was characteristic of the earliest Lodekkas. Service 271 traversed some of the more spectacular stretches of the Isle of Purbeck's southern shore. *Peter J. Relf*

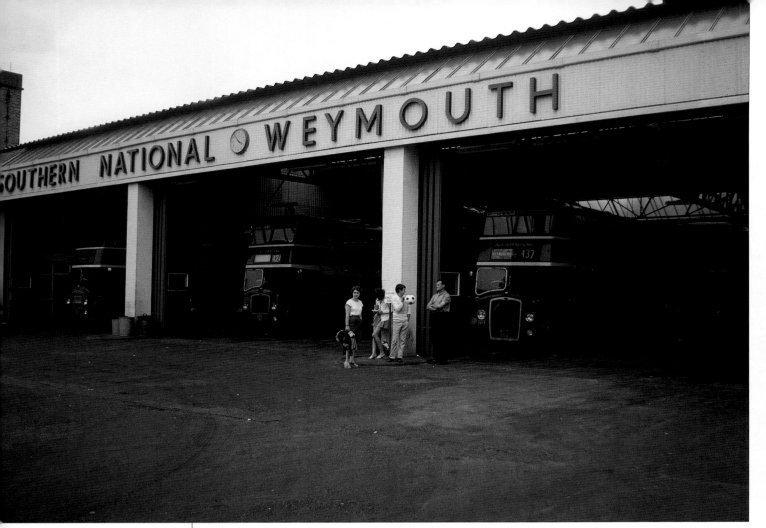

*Above:* It was not until 1958 that the finishing touches were eventually applied to the rebuilt and updated version of the Edward Street garage in Weymouth. Of the three Bristol Lodekkas at the entrances, the nearest, No 1877 (RTT 996) of 1955 displays the earlier-type deep grille to its cowled front.
*DWR Picture Library*

*Right:* Vintage scene. Two Bristol LWL6B/ECW 39-seater saloons stand at the entrance to the rebuilt Edward Street garage. They couldn't have done that when they were new in 1951; Nos 1600 (LTA 935) and 1603 (LTA 972) were delivered well before that job was completed.
*DWR Picture Library*

*Left:* Approaching Paris Street bus station, Exeter, on route 146 from Bideford via Winkleigh and Crediton is No 1900 (TUO 501), one of a batch of 13 60-seat Bristol LD6B/ECW Lodekkas, with rear doors, delivered to Southern National in 1956. *Mike J. Stephens*

*Below:* Turning into Churchfield Road on its final approach to Appledore, Bristol LD6B/ECW Lodekka No 1909 (UOD 492) of 1956 is completing a journey from Bideford. In the background is the estuary of the River Torridge. *Mike J. Stephens*

*Above:* The flat front of the Bristol LS/ECW saloon was seized upon by the company (and WN) to advertise itself in letters large. By a trick of the skylights at Edward Street Nos 1682 (LTA 979) and 1700 (OTT 54) appear to be painted in Southdown colours. *DWR Picture Library*

*Left:* The introduction of the full-fronted, front-entrance Bristol LS brought a more spacious yet 45-seat capacity into use with Southern National. This is the interior of No 1701 (OTT 55), an LS5G with the standard ECW bodywork. *DWR Picture Library*

*Below:* Already with screen set for a short journey to St Eval Camp along route 171, Bristol LS No 1765 (RTT 984) of 1956 awaits its place in Newquay bus station on layover in the company of a Bristol K in St Michaels Road. *Mike J. Stephens*

*Above:* Shining in the sun outside Lynton 'dormy' shed is No 1787 (VDV 788), a 1958 Bristol MW5G/ECW saloon whose seating capacity had been reduced from 45 to 41 the following year. It awaits a turn to Ilfracombe via Blackmore Gate.
*Mike J. Stephens*

*Right:* The driver catches up on the daily news while on layover at Wadebridge on 8 June 1962. In his charge is No 612 (668 COD), a Bristol SUS4A small-capacity saloon of 1960, with 30-seat bodywork by ECW. He is about to return the vehicle safely to Bude via the romantically scenic Atlantic Coast route 122 via Tintagel and Boscastle. *R. B. Partridge*

*Left:* On 30 July 1966 Bristol LS5G No 1685 (LTA 982) stands by at Swanage 'departure station' (sounds vaguely American!) for a journey to Edward Street, Weymouth, via Corfe Castle and Wareham on service 28 — a route established by the National Omnibus & Transport Co as its 36.
*C. L. Caddy*

*Right and below:* An essay in contrasting styles: two Bristol SUL4A/ECW 33-seat coaches delivered in 1961 and just three fleet numbers apart. No 406 (316 EDV) was caught on camera at Taunton while providing a Royal Blue 'relief' to London on 4 June 1966, whilst No 409 (923 GUO) was being shunted at Portland on 26 March 1968.
*C. L. Caddy*

On the plus side, May 1968 saw a new central bus and coach station opened in Earl Street, Yeovil, replacing half a dozen termini scattered throughout the town.

The Transport Act 1962 had already dis-membered the British Transport Commission, marking the final separation of road and rail interests; that was as much as Harold MacMillan's Conservative Government was able to achieve in that direction. Within that decade the political pendulum had swung in the opposite direction. Labour's Transport Minister, Barbara Castle, master-minded the nationalisation of the remainder of the territorial bus industry. On 22 November 1967 the British Electric Traction Co announced its reluctant agreement to the sale to the BTC's successor, the Transport Holding Co, of its UK bus operations (these included Devon General, long sandwiched in the midst of 'nationalised' National).

The path was now clear to set up the ultimate form of road-passenger-transport nationalisation. The Transport Act 1968 incorporated by statute the National Bus Company — a nationwide organisation which held as its subsidiaries 41 bus companies eventually obliged to wear one of two available common liveries — washed-out green or red — a fate which the Southern National Omnibus Co's vehicles were, by not-too-distant events, spared. In 1969 the share capital of Western National and Southern National, together with that of the other 39 subsidiaries, was transferred to the National Bus Company. The last remnant of association with British Rail was severed.

In a complete reversal of the scenario three decades previously, when Western National 'owned' Bristol Tramways & Carriage Co Ltd, J. T. E. Robinson of the (now) Bristol Omnibus Co Ltd became Managing Director of WN/SN as from 1 January 1970. It had already decided — at last — that Southern National's operations should become fully integrated with those of Western National. The assets of Southern National, together with the accounts, had been transferred to Western National in October/November 1969. For administrative purposes this was backdated to 1 January 1969. The Southern National *company* itself had not become part of Western National, nor was it wound up. Instead, in the words of the Kithead Trust's Peter Jaques, it had 'gone into NBC's locker'. However, Southern National vehicles, until receiving 'Western' fleetnames, had been displaying 'Western National' in their destination screen apertures whilst on service in the last year.

Just as Company No 155374 (Devon General) was passed on by NBC for further use by one of its new saleable subsidiaries under the Conservatives, so that of Southern National was sent north to formalise a newly constituted entity. United Auto-mobile Services having been split into two and a bit parts, one of these, Northumbria Motor Services Ltd, received that number, a certificate of change of name being issued by Companies House on 4 July 1986. On 2 April 1998 another such certificate was issued, Company No 237558 being renamed Arriva Northumbria Ltd, under which title, it currently (2007) still trades, far from its original home.

Yeovil enquiry office in 1969. No 2700 (HDV 626E) was SN's first Bristol RELL saloon — with 53 seats and six-cylinder Gardner engine, whilst No 724 (MUO 336F) was one of the company's first examples of the Bristol LH — with 41 seats and a six-cylinder Leyland engine. Both had been delivered in the summer of 1967.
*DWR Picture Library*

*Above:* In one of those rare coups for the photographer, Southern National's first Bristol LH (left) and first Bristol RE saloon are captured side by side at the company's Reckleford property in Yeovil. *DWR Picture Library*

*Below:* Not an altogether ideal site for a depot. A reliable handbrake and gearbox must have been a must for SN employees' cars parked outside. The Reckleford garage in Yeovil, with the original Petters yard at the rear, which provided a major parking space for buses. *DWR Picture Library*

Negotiating the ascent to Tophill, on the Isle of Portland, *en route* to Easton, at the centre of the island, Bristol RELL6G/ECW 53-seater saloon No 2705 (HDV 631E) is pictured against the spectacular backdrop of Chesil Beach and Portland Harbour. The 22F variation of this route commenced operation in 1954. *C. L. Caddy*

...TH COVE
...030

...Dorchester
...ntry", passing
...Hardy. Arrive
...lunch and si...
...hours for tea a...
...through Abbot...

...& CHEDD...
...0930

...ne and Ilchester
...bbey Ruins. Proc
...and viewing the
...made through
...aves. Return via
...ur is made for tea...

...AY
...0930

...d. Clyst St. Mary
...ur. Proceed via T
...y, arriving at app...
...and sightseeing.
...Hill, Exeter, wher...
...on and Axminster.

...R ROCKS &
...1000

...rd, Newton Popple
...y Tracey. Stop 1½ h
...seeing. Return via
...e, Exeter (stop 1
...r.

...OUTH & MI...
...g 0930

...inster and Honiton
...through the Exe Valle
...d Watersmeet. Stop 1½
...eing and a trip on the
...ehead (where a stop
...n, Chard and Axminster...

...KFASTLEIGH
...ng 1000

## 42. MINEHEAD & THE EXE VALLEY     17/6
*Leaving 0945*

Via Axminster, Chard, Taunton and Williton to Minehead.
Stop for lunch and sightseeing. Return via Dunster and
down the Exe Valley via Tiverton to Exeter (stop 1 hour
for tea) and Sidford.

...& TEIGNMOUTH     14/6

...hour at Dalish, then for lunch and sight-
...th. Returning via Exeter (stop 1 hour for
...Axminster.

...ZOO     15/-

...½ hour), Newton Abbot and Totnes.
...15 and return via Torquay, Teignmouth
..., Exeter and Honiton.

...     15/6
(Coach Fare only)

...Teignmouth, Torquay and Paignton to
...via Totnes, Newton Abbot and Exeter.
...be operated in the reverse direction
...es of the River Dart Steamboats.

...& PORTLAND     14/-

...otsbury. Stop at Weymouth from 1130
...d Island and depart Portland Bill at 1645
...and Bridport.

...OUSE &
          SHEARWATER     17/6

### BATH & BRISTOL ZOO
**Leaving Southwell 0900, Weymouth ...
and Dorchester (Top O'Town) 09...**

Via Dorchester, Sherborne, Castle Cary, S...
Keynsham, returning same route. Arrive Do...
2000 and Southwell 2030.

### DARTMOOR
**Leaving Southwell 0900, Weymouth ...
and Dorchester (Top O'Town) 09...**

...his tour takes one through a vast expa...
...r its beauty and grandeur. Places o...
...where a stop of 1 hour is made for lun...
...stbridge, Princetown Tavistock and
...orchester 2045, Weymouth 2100 and So...

### WELLS, CHEDDAR & WES...
MARE
**Leaving Southwell 0900, Weymouth ...
and Dorchester (Top O'Town) 09...**

The route takes one through Sherborne,
Shepton Mallet and Wells, where 1½ hou...
and to view the Cathedral. Proceed to C...
an hour is made at Weston-super-Mare...
Returning via Bridgwater and Taunton.
Weymouth 2030 and Southwell 2100.

### PORTSMOUTH & SOUTHS...
**Leaving Southwell 0900, Weymouth ...
and Dorchester (Museum) 0945**

Here is a Day-Tour offering both coasta...
through Wimborne, Ringwood and the
mouth, where a stop of 3 hours is made f...
Returning via Christchurch, Bournem...
Dorchester. Arrive Dorchester 2045. Weymouth 2100 and Southwell
2130.

## 50. BUDE     21/-
*Leaving 0930*

Via Exeter, stop 1045-1115, Okehampton and Hatherleigh.
Arrive Bude 1330. Depart 1445 proceed via Bideford to
Barnstaple. Stop 1615–1715. Return via Tiverton,
Cullompton, Honiton and Axminster, arriving Lyme Regis
2000.

## 52. BOURNEMOUTH     16/6
*Leaving 0930*

Via Dorchester, Wareham, Swanage Studland Ferry and
Branksome Chine. Arrive Bournemouth 1230. Depart 1645
and return via Bere Regis and Dorchester.

## 55. WEYMOUTH     10/-
*Leaving 1000*

Via Bridport and Abbotsbury. Arrive Weymouth 1145.
Depart 1645 and return via Dorchester, where a stop of
½ hour is made, and Bridport.

63.

66.

# TOURS & EXCURSIONS
FROM **LYME REGIS**
BY **" SOUTHERN NATIONAL "**

# TOURS & EXCURSIONS
FROM **WEYMOUTH**
**DORCHESTER, SOUTHWELL
AND ISLE OF PORTLAND**
BY **" SOUTHERN NATIONAL "**

Blenheim Palace,
place of Sir Wins...
Ringwood and Wi...

LECTION OF

ALF-DAY

URY
30
urton Brad
vs of Chesil
stop at Ab
vannery. R
t, Chideock

TH
430
nd Sidfor
1730,
niton and

& B
430
and
0 for
same

M B
1415
, Ne
at 1
m Co

SELECTION OF POPULAR

## WHOLE DAY TOURS

*These Tours arrive back at approximately 1845 unless otherwise stated.*

### 4. PENZANCE, LAND'S END & ST. IVES

Leaving 0830 — 25/–

*Via* Camelford, Wadebridge and Truro. Stop $\frac{1}{4}$ hour. From Truro *via* Fraddon and Redruth to Penzance. Stop 1 hour for lunch and sightseeing. Proceed to Land's End. Stop $\frac{3}{4}$ hour. Return along the coast road to St. Ives. Stop $\frac{3}{4}$ hour for tea. Then *via* Redruth, Wadebridge (stop $\frac{1}{4}$ hour) and Camelford. Home 2000.

### 5. PAIGNTON & BUCKFAST ABBEY

Leaving 0930 — 17/–

*Via* Holsworthy, Hatherleigh, Okehampton and Moretonhampstead; stop $\frac{1}{4}$ hour. Then *via* Bovey Tracey, Newton Abbot and Torquay to Paignton, stop $1\frac{1}{2}$ hours for lunch. Returning *via* Totnes and Buckfastleigh; stop $\frac{1}{2}$ hour at Buckfast Abbey, then on to Dartmeet, stop for sightseeing, etc., and over Dartmoor: then *via* Tavistock and Launceston.

### 10. ILFRACOMBE

Leaving 0930 — 14/–

*Via* Bideford and Barnstaple. Stop at Bideford $\frac{1}{2}$ hour and $2\frac{1}{4}$ hours at Ilfracombe. Returning *via* the same route, a stop is made at Barnstaple for $1\frac{1}{2}$ hours.

### 14. DOONE VALLEY

Leaving 0930 — 18/–

*Via* Bideford, Barnstaple; stop $\frac{1}{2}$ hour; Brendon, Malmesmead. Stop $1\frac{1}{2}$ hours for lunch and sightseeing. Return *via* Lynmouth, Blackmoor Gate, Combe Marti...
stop 1 hour for tea...

### 16. LYNTON & LYNMOUTH

Leaving 0930 — 15/6

*Via* Bideford and Barnstaple to Lynton. Stops of $\frac{1}{2}$ hour at Bideford and $2\frac{3}{4}$ hours at Lynton. Returning *via* the Valley of Rocks to Barnstaple; stop $\frac{3}{4}$ hour. Then *via* Bideford.

### 29. FALMOUT...

Leaving 09...

*Via* Camelford, ...
at Wadebridge f...
ing *via* Castle Dr...
with a stop at T...

### 30. FOWEY

Leaving 0...

*Via* Launceston...
at Bodmin and...
Austell, Mevag...
$1\frac{3}{4}$ hours at M...

### 31. WOOLA...

Leaving ...

*Via* Stratton...
Barnstaple, B...
Stops of $\frac{1}{4}$ ho...
Returning *vi*...
hour at Ilfrac...

### 33. DARTM...

Leaving ...

*Via* Holswor...
hampstead...

# TOURS AND EXCURSIONS

FROM **BUDE** AND **STRATTON**

BY **"SOUTHERN NATIONAL"**

SELECTIO...

## HALF-D...

*These Tours arrive ba...*

### ...ORWENSTO...

...aving 1415

... Stratton and Kilkham...
...hampton Church for $\frac{1}{2}$...
...wing time to visit Ha...
...ey. Stop $1\frac{1}{2}$ hours befor...
...k 1830 approximately.

### ...REBARWITH

...eaving 1415

... Tintagel to Trebarwith;
...scastle, Tresparret Post...
...idemouth Bay. Stop at Bos...

### ...INTAGEL & BO...

...eaving 1415

...a Widemouth Bay, Coppatho...
...tch Barrow to Tintagel; sto...
...oscastle and Tresparret Posts.

### MOORLAND TOUR

Leaving 1415

*Via* Otterham Station, Hallwor...
...nn and Dozmary Pool. Stops ...
Dozmary for $\frac{1}{4}$ hour. Returning ...
stop of $1\frac{1}{2}$ hours is made.

### POLZEATH SANDS

Leaving 1415

*Via* Widemouth Bay, Camelford...
Polzeath; stop $1\frac{3}{4}$ hours. Return...
Delabole, Camelford Station and S...

### PORT ISAAC & POR...

Leaving 1415

**W. 9/6**
**...nouth 1030 — P.11/–**
**...045 — D. 7/6**
...hester, Bere Regis, Wimborne, ...dhurst to Beaulieu Abbey. The Montagu of Beaulieu. Return *via* ...emouth (stop for tea), Bere ...chester 1915, Weymouth 1930

**W.20/–**
**...eymouth 0900 — P.20/6**
...ey, Winchester, Basingstoke and ...gstoke, Stockbridge, Salisbury, Weymouth 2130 and Southwell

**W.20/–**
**...eymouth 0830 — P.20/6**
... and coastal scenery. *Via* Wim- ... Forest to Fareham, Arundel and ... Fareham, Lyndhurst and Bourne- ...d Southwell 2230.

**W.21/–**
**...mouth 0900 — P.21/6**
**...wn) 0915 — D.19/–**
...er, Bridport, Honiton, Exeter and ..., Okehampton, Exeter, Honiton, ...orchester 2115, Weymouth 2130

**...EM — W.20/–**
**P.20/–**
**...Veymouth 0900**
...over, Newbury and Oxford to ... Duke of Marlborough and birth- ... Return *via* Newbury, Salisbury, ... Weymouth 2200 and Southwell

**ALL TOURS START FROM ...**
**(Edward Street)**

Passengers may also be picked up on certa... (Eight Kings), EASTON (Square), FO... Offices), PORTLAND (Victoria Square... Hotel), WEYMOUTH (St. John's Churc... OVERCOMBE CORNER, RIVERA CA... BURY LODGE, PRESTON (Ship Inn), ... Hotel), OSMINGTON CHALET CAMP a... CAMP. For details enquire at the Compa...
Seats may be booked in advance w... Company's Local Offices: **5 ROYAL ... WEYMOUTH; OMNIBUS ... STREET, WEYMOUTH** (Tel. Weymouth 3645/6) or ... the Company's Local Agents:

**Mr. PILKINGTON, Confectioner, WAKEHAM**
**Mr. P. READ, Hairdresser, 87 Fortuneswell, PORTLAND**
**Mrs. DICKINSON, 58 Portland Road, WYKE REGIS**

Seats may also be booked in advance without extra charge at **THE DORCHESTER TRAVEL AGENCY, 55 High West Street, DORCHESTER.** (Tel. Dorchester 1748).

SELECTION OF POPULAR

## HALF-DAY TOURS

W—Fares from Weymouth.
P—Fares from Southwell, Portland and Wyke Regis.
D—Fares from Dorchester.

**CORFE CASTLE & SWANAGE — W. 7/–**
**Leaving Southwell 1400 and Weymouth 1430 — P. 8/6**
*Via* Preston, Osmington, Wool and Wareham. Return *via* Wareham, Bere Regis and Moreton Heath. Arrive back 1830.

**PORTLAND BILL — W. 4/9**
**Leaving Weymouth 1430**

*Above:* Parked beside the River Camel at Padstow, No 1775 (TUO 491), a 1956 Bristol LS5G, awaits a return journey to Newquay along the B3276 via Trenance on route 171. Despite the 'Western National' blind this was very much an SN route on 4 August 1968. *Mike J. Stephens*

*Right:* Bound for Littlemoor, Bristol KSW6B/ECW 55-seater No 1844 (LTA 954) takes the Wareham Road upon leaving Weymouth (the other lane goes around in a curve) on 22 February 1969. NBC was by then in control, and plans to subsume Southern National within Western National would see the route number (33B) altered within a matter of months. *C. L. Caddy*

*Above:* One of the latter-day deliveries to a still-extant Southern National Omnibus Co Ltd was this Bristol RELH6G/ECW 45-seater, 1461 (OTA 633G), which, with a semi-automatic gearbox, made the driver's life so much easier. It is pictured on layover at Bideford Quay in the company of two Western National vehicles. *DWR Picture Library*

*Left:* Parked in Exeter's Paris Street bus station, at a spot where one might expect to see instead a red Devon General vehicle, is No 731 (POD 802H), the last Bristol LH6L delivered to Southern National. It has arrived in Exeter from Bideford displaying a WN route number. *DWR Picture Library*

*Above:* Looking good in Yeovil bus station is No 1848 (LTA 991), a Bristol KSW6B/ECW of 1952. The KSW was the 8ft-wide development of the earlier KS model. The date is 21 June 1969, and the vehicle is already displaying the new 'Western National' route number (460) imposed in lieu of Southern National's 1 for this Yeovil local service. *C. L. Caddy*

*Right:* Still identifying itself as a Southern National, No 1833 (LTA 943), one of the first KSW models in either National fleet, entered service in 1950. On 21 June 1969 it was on its way to Yeovil's Milford Estate, on a short working upon what was previously SN service 1B. The KSW was the Tilling Association's response to a national campaign to give passengers 'a wider seat'. *C. L. Caddy*

*Left:* It is 30 July 1969, and a Southern National vehicle is now further 'Westernised'. In addition to the alteration of its service number (435) from what had been the Southern National 33, the upper blind now declares the bus to be a 'Western National'. No 1875 (RTT 994) was a Bristol LD6B/ECW 58-seater delivered in 1955. *C. L. Caddy*

*Left:* Pictured at Yeovil on 2 August 1969, with blind set for a journey to points east of Sherborne on what would previously have been SN service 12, No 1713 (OTT 67) was now a Western National vehicle in waiting. A 1954 Bristol LS6G/ECW saloon new in 1954 with 39 seats, it had been upseated to 41 in 1959 for OMO use. *C. L. Caddy*

*Above:* A wide variety of coaches lurk in the background as Bristol LS6G coach No 1380 (OTT 69) departs Yeovil Town station in August 1969, passing a parked Bristol KSW on layover between journeys on service 469 (Yeovil–Milborne Port), previously SN route 12. *DWR Picture Library*

*Upper right:* Latter-day Southern National. As the last days of summer in 1969 came to a close, so too did the operational days of the Southern National company. Here a Bristol FLF6G/ECW 68-seater, No 1977 (465 FTT) of 1961, negotiates a large roundabout on the A30 whilst working a Yeovil town service. *DWR Picture Library*

*Right:* Looking rather lonely in Exeter's Paris Street bus station in July 1969, No 1900 (TUO 501) shows off its rear-door configuration. A 1956 Bristol LD6B/ECW Lodekka, the vehicle was on layover before returning to Bideford — with WN-series service number. *DWR Picture Library*

*Left:* "We'm still Southern National as far as I'm concerned! "The driver of No 1849 (LTA 992), perhaps defiantly, has scrolled up the old firm's name for a journey on 'Western National' route 437 (if that's the right number) to Wyke Regis. The bus was photographed crossing the River Wey on 17 September 1969. *C.L.Caddy*

*Below:* New in 1948 as a Royal Blue coach, Bristol L6B No 1224 (JUO 989) was lengthened and given this replacement full-fronted 39-seat ECW body in 1958. The vehicle was photographed in Newquay, working the ex-SN 172 route to St Mawgan (now Western National 623), in 1969. *DWR Picture Library*

*Above:* Bristol LS5G
No 1699 (OTT 53) leaves
Weymouth's Edward Street
bus station *en route* for
Littlesea Caravan Camp in
the autumn of 1969.
What used to be service 61B
has now become 443 in the
Western National series.
*DWR Picture Library*

*Right:* Dramatic Cornish
scenery near the coast at
Boscastle is the setting for
Bristol LS5G No 1768
(RTT 987), running from
Bude to Wadebridge via
Tintagel on what used to be
SN service 122 but which
has now been taken into
the WN services as 322.
*DWR Picture Library*

*Left:* The end of the line. A far cry from the day in July 1930 when that busy little Southern Railway 'T1' tank engine stood on this very spot: Bristol MW5G/ECW 45-seat saloon No 2623 (754 MDV) is parked upon that post-Beeching dereliction which was Swanage railway station in 1967. Fortunately for those of us who care about such things, a praiseworthy group have restored the line — but the Southern National Omnibus Co Ltd was put to sleep at the close of 1969. *Alec Swain*

*Left:* Despite the fleetname on the front of the bus, the Southern National Omnibus Co Ltd had already become a dormant company, subsumed under Western National, by the time this picture was taken on Weymouth seafront. As a colleague approaches, the driver of No 1014 (705 JHY) closes his door with almost symbolic finality. The vehicle, ex Bristol Omnibus Co in 1967, was a Bristol FSF6G/ECW 60-seater on a short local-service duty — numbered 20A! *Alan O. Watkins*

*Above:* At Edward Street, Weymouth, is No 1014 (705 JHY), one of eight ex-Bristol Omnibus Co Bristol FSFs acquired by Southern National in 1967. Although not liked over much by SN crews they featured a forward-entrance and a Cave-Browne-Cave heating/ventilation system, as revealed by the two intakes on either side of the destination display. *DWR Picture Library*

*Left:* Route 119 from Bideford to Bude became the 319 in Western National days, which began in 1969. Bristol LS5G No 1767 (RTT 986) of 1956 had been converted from 45-seat to 41-seat OMO configuration in 1958. The bus — still with Southern National fleetnames — is seen at Bideford depot in 1972. *DWR Picture Library*

*Below:* A Bristol SUL4A/ECW coach looms large in the well-lit interior of Boutport Street garage in Barnstaple, the site of which was bought by Southern National in 1936. An interesting mix of Bristol/ECW types accompany the coach. *DWR Picture Library*

*Left:* A surviving Southern Railway notice on the approach road to Yeovil Town station and one of several Royal Blue coaches flank No 2065 (BOD 25C), a Bristol FLF6B/ECW 70-seater. A field nearby was used on Saturdays for express service exchange purposes. *DWR Picture Library*

*Below:* Well into NBC and Western National ownership, No 690 (EDV 553D), a Bristol SUL4A/ECW 36-seat saloon that began life in 1966 with Southern National, is pictured on active service at Netherbury, in deepest Dorset. It has to be said that its leaf-green livery blends well with the beautiful landscape. *DWR Picture Library*

# Express Services /
# Royal Blue

IT COULD be said that National's involvement in express services can be traced back to its decision in 1919 to hang on to its Becklow Road Garage in Shepherd's Bush, at the time when it relinquished its London stage-carriage services in favour of the LGOC. The latter had agreed that the National Steam Car Co Ltd could retain it to house up to an initial 10 vehicles, sufficient to maintain a presence in West London for the purpose of continuing the relatively small excursions and private-hire department. Over the next decade that fleet crept up to 27.

AEC YC chassis fitted with 28-seat charabanc bodies did duty in that role into the early 1920s, albeit when not being transmogrified into single or double-deck stage-carriage vehicles for use in the provinces. The first use of the Shepherd's Bush premises as a base for what later became known as 'express services' came in that year of 1919, when the National Union of Railwaymen called a nationwide strike in response to the Lloyd George Government's proposal to reduce its members' wages. In the event the Government soon acceded to the railwaymen's terms, but in the interim several charabanc owners discovered that getting stranded passengers into and out of London led to a considerable amount of continuing loyalty toward this alternative mode of travel. Among the firms which provided facilities that September were Southdown, Elliott Bros of Bournemouth (see *Glory Days: Royal Blue*) and National. Since the last had not yet established itself in the West Country, National's charabancs were restricted to journeys between London and destinations in Essex. Nevertheless, much had been learned.

In 1920, with numerous proprietors entering the field and offering charabanc trips upon a competitive basis from the capital to the coast, Mr Shirley James, Charabanc Manager of Pickford's Ltd, came to the conclusion that an exclusive 'pool' should be formed to enable its participants to help each other out, and several London-based firms joined forces with two from the provinces (Southdown and East Kent). National's contribution seems to have been formalised in 1923 with the founding proper of London & Coastal Coaches. For some 10 years afterward National referred to its Shepherd's Bush contribution to this activity as its 'London & Coastal Business'.

As more and more passengers sought to take advantage of the increasing facilities now being offered the decision was taken to recast control of the organisation into a limited-liability company. On 5 May 1925 London Coastal Coaches Ltd held its first board meeting. The National Omnibus & Transport Co Ltd was host to that gathering, which appointed National's Bert Smith as Chairman and Secretary. Appropriately the registered office was located within National's headquarters at 206 Brompton Road, Kensington, SW3. By now National had gained important coastal footholds in the West Country that had become popular destinations for such long-distance work.

The plan at the outset had included measures to get the coaches at the London end into a centralised departure point. This proved more difficult than expected, and it was not until April 1928 that a rudimentary 2-acre site — originally intended to house a tramways power station — was found off Lupus Street, near Vauxhall Bridge. It was from here that the all-weather coaches of National, Elliott Bros' Royal Blue and, later, the sun-saloons of Southern National and Western National jostled for space and raised the dust (or splattered off through the puddles and mud) as they set out for those romantic holiday destinations in the West Country.

When, in 1929, National and the appropriate railway companies agreed to the formation of three new National operating entities each newly appointed board began to take a sharpened look at the opposition in its respective area. In Southern National's case it had inherited the North Devon area, long served also by George Samuelson's express coaches. It became aware that Silver Cars of Seaton — on the South Devon coast — had started a new express service to London in conjunction with Samuelson's. Southern National was to make an offer for Silver Cars in 1932 but failed to acquire it until March 1935. During the summer of 1930 the Great Western Railway was still operating its 'Land Cruises' through Southern National's territory, but the SR representatives on the board thought it politic not to object.

The National Omnibus & Transport Co., LTD..
SHEPHERDS BUSH.

_____ 192

This is to certify that I have this day paid into the **London County Westminster & Parrs Bank Ltd., Shepherds Bush**, to the credit of the above Company, " a/c Camberwell Branch," the sum of

£ : s. d. as follows :

Total £

BANK RECEIPT.

_____ Cashier.

Firm No 198 H.C.&Co., 15162. 500. 11/30.

*Right:* By 1925 the cape-cart-hooded charabanc was becoming decidedly dated and was no longer popular save on the warmest days of summer. In addition customers were beginning to patronise the smaller pneumatic-tyred coaches coming into service with competing independents. Accordingly AEC YC No 2046 (HK 7244), here parked up in Bridport, soon afterward became an open-top double-decker bus.
*The Omnibus Society*

*Below:* Weymouth was set to become a very popular destination for express services from London. Locally based Edward W. Puffett had already given the port a taste of travel by charabanc with this 1913 Thornycroft C-type 20-seater (FX 1871). Operating from the yard of the former horse-drawn Weymouth Omnibus Co, Puffett was also an early operator of a motorised stage-carriage service. *Hugh Bannister collection*

*Below:* Still wearing its original Silver Cars livery, Leyland Tiger TS1 No 3545 (DV 1072) rolls up ready for its customary Seaton–London express duty in August 1935. Together with nine other coaches from that fleet it had been the property of Southern National for some two months.
*The Omnibus Society*

Meanwhile, what to do with National's 'London & Coastal Business'? It was decided that it was down to the GWR and SR as to how the express services to the west should be operated — a merger with Western National and Southern National respectively, or by the formation of a new company? In the interim it was decided to pool the whole of the receipts for an initial, trial period to 30 September 1930, whilst Southern National prepared to issue agreed preference shares, in what could well become its portion, to the SR, it being agreed Western National should have first choice (in selecting 11) of the 22 coaches 'going west'. The remaining part of the London & Coastal Business, including five coaches, was to go to the Eastern National Omnibus Co Ltd.

By December 1930 Southern National had title to its section of the London business at the agreed price of £21,500, together with 319 shares of £1

each in London Coastal Coaches Ltd. In 1932 it was discussed whether the operation and maintenance of the London fleet should be placed under the control of Tilling, but, in the event, NO&T retained day-to-day control on behalf of its subsidiaries. Just how much influence the relative railway representatives held was demonstrated by the appointment of SR's Herbert Short to be Southern National's nominee on the newly established Management Committee of the London & Coastal business — and by the fact that proposed new express services or those to be converted from stage-carriage status had first to be submitted for SR approval. That the 22 'south west' vehicles were largely operated seasonally is underlined by the fact that most of them were stored for the winter months at the Chiswick Motor Co's garage — all at £8 per week.

Bert Smith was of the opinion that it would be cheaper to discontinue the use of London as the centre for garaging and to transfer the coaches to the local depots of the respective companies. 'Oh no!' said the SN board. 'We'd lose the private-hire and special trip work in London.' By 1933, however, it was beginning to look as though Smith had been right. Whilst, by and large, the fleet was serviceable, a number of the coaches still had the old-type 'all-weather' cape-cart hoods, which did not compare at all favourably with their competitors — modern sun-saloons with luxurious seating. It was estimated that it would cost £21,317 to bring the London fleet up to scratch.

The pool of the London & Coastal Business was dissolved on 31 March 1933 — and just as well, because Elliott Bros (Bournemouth) Ltd was now advertising connections at Yeovil for London passengers travelling to Ilfracombe. Instead, arrangements were made with Elliott's Royal Blue for a working and pooling scheme for London–Bournemouth and London–Plymouth

services operated by SN, WN and Elliott Bros, the last using impressive new vehicles. Control at the London end was now assumed by the individual companies, with a joint booking office at National's 206 Brompton Road.

From the 1933 season Southern National ran express services from London's year-old Victoria Coach Station to Ilfracombe, Bideford, Barnstaple, Lynton, Swanage and Weymouth — the fares to the last two being the same at 12s 6d (62p) single and 22s 6d (£1.12) return — whilst Western National ran to Penzance and to Newquay. Following the joint purchase of those services in their respective areas previously operated by Highways (1933) Ltd and Highways (Bournemouth) Ltd, WN/SN agreed a working arrangement was with Elliott Bros' Royal Blue whereby they took 46% and Elliott Bros 54% on the all-year-round London–Plymouth route; WN/SN received 20% and Elliotts 80% of the total receipts on the London–Southampton–Bournemouth–Torquay–Paignton service during the summer period, when the WN/SN licences were valid, the same proportionate mileage having been run by each operator.

Elsewhere, the Western and Southern Traffic Commissioners refused to grant licences for a proposed joint WN/SN express service between Cheltenham and Weymouth. In May 1934, as a small consolation, WN/SN made a joint £400 purchase of the London service operated by Reginald Austin's Greyhound Coaches, of Weymouth. That summer, however, there commenced a process of acquisition which was to change the public image of Western National's and Southern National's express operations — one which has never been matched, and which was to last until the 1970s when the National Bus Company (no, not the NO&T but the 'politically nationalised' one) began to bleach the colour out of it. In July 1934 National representatives paid an

No 3110 (DR 8525) was one of a pair of Leyland Tiger TS1 coaches purchased by Southern National in 1931. Both chassis were in William Mumford's body shop at the same time as two Thornycrofts and the solitary Reo FB, completed as stage-carriage saloons. No 3110, however, was destined for rather more upmarket work — excursions, tours and periodic use on express and limited-stop services. *Ian Allan Library*

official visit to John and Harry Elliott at Holdenhurst Road, Bournemouth. It was Southern National which, on 23 November, offered to buy Elliott Bros (Bournemouth) Ltd for £122,500. The following month Elliott's licences had been applied for, were granted, and the business purchased jointly with Western National in equal shares.

As the headquarters of Hants & Dorset Motor Services Ltd was located in Bournemouth, and as H&D had been until then precluded by a 1924 agreement with Elliott Bros from running excursions and tours, that aspect of Royal Blue activities passed to Hants & Dorset. The express-service work, however, was acquired by Western National and Southern National, the goodwill of Elliott Bros being divided ⅜ to Hants & Dorset and ⅝ to Western/Southern National conjointly. Western National took nominal control of Royal Blue's Rutland Road works in Bournemouth, whilst the garage in the same location became the property of Southern National. Hants & Dorset acquired various leasehold properties in Bournemouth and Royal Blue's garage in Yarmouth, Isle of Wight. Hants & Dorset also transferred the rental of the lower portion of its Bournemouth bus and coach station in The Square from Elliott Bros to both National companies for £1,000 each per annum plus their proportion of the local council rates.

For those who have not read *Glory Days: Royal Blue* (2000), Elliott Bros Royal Blue had been founded at Bournemouth in 1880, when Thomas Elliott was granted a hackney-carriage-driver's licence. He acquired his first carriage (a landau) in

1885 and his first replica stage coach in 1894 (there being no real ones left on the road at that time) and built up a reputation for good organisation and presentation. Tom Elliott died in 1911, and thereafter the firm became Elliott Bros, his sons. They bought their first two motor cabs in October 1912 and their first two motor charabancs (Dennis 20-seaters) in March 1913.

Knocked back by the requisition of British-made chassis in World War 1 and the call-up for military service of his brothers, John 'Jack' Elliott, together with his mother, Elizabeth, kept the firm going with imported American Selden chassis. Postwar the expansion of the firm can only be described as remarkable. At a time when 27 touring licences were held, the 1919 railway strike provided Elliott Bros with the opportunity already mentioned. By 1922 Royal Blue held 55 of the 85 licences granted locally to Bournemouth coach proprietors. In 1927 the firm had been granted membership of London Coastal Coaches Ltd, and the following year it adopted the trading name 'Royal Blue Automobile Services'. Throughout its motorised existence the Royal Blue fleet had been dressed in pale blue. It was a batch of 26 elegant ADC 424 coaches that entered service in the restored dark-blue livery beloved of Tom Elliott. This version was to survive upon Royal Blue coaches — both Elliott Bros and Southern/Western National — for a further half century.

Both the National and Hants & Dorset companies were in the process of ordering new rolling stock in Royal Blue livery whilst another three-way purchase was being arranged — that of

Thomas Elliott, founder of Royal Blue, was granted a licence to drive a horse-drawn cab in 1880. He acquired his own first vehicle — a landau — in 1885 and purchased the first of his four 24-seat replica stage coaches in April 1894. All bar four passengers usually found places at roof level — a top-heavy arrangement, but the local authority saw fit to licence them. His sons ran this one for some five years after his death in 1911.
*Colin Morris collection*

# SAFETY FIRST.

Mess<sup>rs</sup> ELLIOTT BROS., (Bournemouth) L<sup>TD</sup>

Head Booking & Registered Office:— 68, HOLDENHURST RD., BOURNEMOUTH.

**ROYAL EB BLUE**
SAFETY — BOURNEMOUTH. — FIRST
PULCHRITUDO ET SALUBRITAS

MOTOR COACHES.        & PRIVATE HIRE CARS.

PHONE 1610.

# SAFETY FIRST TOURS.

SAFETY FIRST. This is no catch-word as far as the Royal Blue is concerned—Safety is assured by the drastic thoroughness with which every car is examined and tested by the Royal Blue highly skilled and up-to-date Engineering Department—both before and after every journey. All drivers are skilled men and know the district well—all conductors are certified drivers.

Telephones: 1610, 1611, 1612, (Private Branch Exchange).

THIS FOLDER IS THE COPYRIGHT OF ELLIOTT BROS. (B'MOUTH) LTD.

---

# The Cliffs & Caves of Cheddar VIA Wells Cathedral.

Depart Holdenhurst Road Garage, 8 a.m. Taxi free to Coach. Return Fare, 12/6

FOR this tour to view the finest Inland Cliff Scenery in the Kingdom, we leave Bournemouth via UPPER PARKSTONE, STOUR VALLEY and BLANDFORD, thence through the many old-world villages of the beautiful Blackmore Vale country, including STURMINSTER NEWTON and STALBRIDGE. Crossing the county boundary from Dorset into Somerset, a short halt is made at TEMPLE-COMBE, the journey continuing through WINCANTON and CASTLE CARY. We are now in the most fertile part of rural Somerset. After a delightful spin of about eight miles we reach WELLS, where lunch can be obtained : time being allowed to visit the important Cathedral, which ranges in date from the 12th to the 15th centuries, showing the beautiful West Front of the Cathedral is considered by some authorities to be the finest outdoor sculpture gallery in Europe. Resuming our journey, we make a steady ascent to the top of the Mendip Range, obtaining extensive views, reaching CHEDDAR GORGE. Here the imposing grandeur of the cliffs as they tower about 500 feet perpendicular on either side is truly wonderful. Time is allowed to visit the Cliffs and Caves of Cheddar, which are of the most beautiful. One of the most romantic pieces of scenery it is possible to see. The picture is sublime. One of the most wonderful sights in this region of wonders are those revealed in the Stalactite Caverns. The caverns are pronounced to be the finest in the world. Great geologists and palæontologists have written of them. Magnificent groups, electrically illuminated, present a picture indescribably bewitching. Rivers of sparkling diamonds, lakes of glittering gems, waterfalls of loveliest crystals, rocks snowy white and ruby red as deep-toned as the loveliest music. Leaving Cheddar, we proceed through several pretty Somerset villages to GLASTONBURY, which is noted for its old Abbey Ruins. The Monks' Kitchen is still in an excellent state of preservation. Thence a delightful run across Glastonbury meadows to YEOVIL, where tea is obtained at Messrs. Maynard's Borough Restaurant. Leaving Yeovil, a delightful run through Dorset is made, reaching Bournemouth after one of the finest tours that could be arranged anywhere in England.

A "ROYAL BLUE" WONDER TOUR.

GUARANTEED "DAILY" MOTOR COACH SERVICE

SINGLE FARE 15/-          TO AND FROM

---

**ROYAL EB BLUE**
SAFETY — FIRST

## Afternoon Tours.

Depart Daily (Sundays Included) from the Square and our Lansdowne Booking Office and Holdenhurst Road at 2.30 p.m.

| No. | Tour | Fare |
|---|---|---|
| 12 | TO THE BEAUTIFUL FOREST VILLAGE OF BURLEY | 5/- |
| 25 | LULWORTH COVE | 7/6 |
| 26 | MILTON ABBAS | 6/6 |
| 10 | SWANAGE & CORFE | 7/6 |
| 5 | WIMBORNE MINSTER & CANFORD MODEL VILLAGE | 3/6 |
|  | NEW FOREST, MILFORD-ON-SEA, LYMINGTON, BROCKEN-HURST & LYNDHURST | 7/- |
| 15 | BADBURY RINGS & KINGSTON LACEY | 5/- |
| 16 | NEW FOREST, RUFUS STONE & LYNDHURST | 7/- |
| 11 | CORFE CASTLE & WAREHAM | 5/- |

## Special Afternoon Tours.

Every day (including Sundays) from Lansdowne and the Square, depart 2.30 p.m.

| No. | Tour | Fare |
|---|---|---|
| 32 | SOUTHAMPTON (60 miles through the New Forest) | 6/- |
| 33 | WEYMOUTH (via Wool, and the Dorset Coast) | 6/6 |
| 34 | SALISBURY (via Fordingbridge and Avon Valley) | 6/- |
| 35 | SHAFTESBURY & BLANDFORD | 6/- |
| 36 | LARMER TREE (the most interesting grounds in England) | 6/- |
| 37 | CRANBORNE & FORDINGBRIDGE | 6/- |
| 38 | WORBARROW & CORFE CASTLE | 6/- |
| 39 | STUDLAND & CORFE CASTLE | 6/- |

## Evening Tours.

Depart 6.30 every Evening.

| No. | Tour | Fare |
|---|---|---|
| 40 | *CORFE CASTLE & WAREHAM | 6/- |
| 41 | *BADBURY RINGS & WIMBORNE | 3/6 |
| 42 | *NEW FOREST & BURLEY | 4/- |
| 43 | HIGHCLIFFE & MILFORD-ON-SEA | 3/6 |
| 44 | RINGWOOD via THE RHODODENDRON FOREST | 4/6 |
| 45 | *LYNDHURST & BROCKENHURST | 2/6 |
| 46 | *WIMBORNE MINSTER | 1/6 |
| 47 | *HAVEN & SANDBANKS | |

---

# ROUND THE Isle of Wight

## Complete Motor Tour of the Inland and Coastal Scenery in ONE DAY.

Depart Holdenhurst Road Garage at 7.30 a.m.    Home 6.45 p.m. Taxi free to Coach. Return Fare 12/6

DAILY (SUNDAYS INCLUDED)

STARTING from Lansdowne at 7.30 a.m., we leave the town through BOSCOMBE, passing CHRISTCHURCH, HIGHCLIFFE CASTLE ESTATE, CHEWTON GLEN, MILTON, DOWNTON, NEWLANDS MANOR, EVERTON and PENNINGTON, arriving at LYMINGTON, where we catch a train scheduled at 8.42, which takes us to the Pier Head, where the Southern Railway Boat awaits to convey us across the six miles of the Solent, the total sea journey occupying not more than half an hour. Landing at Yarmouth about 9.30, we allow a wait of 10 minutes. Leaving Yarmouth, we commence our tour of the island on the north-east side, passing through NINGWOOD, SHALFLEET, GUYERS, BARTONS CORNER, SWAINSTON PARK, PARKHURST FOREST, CARISBROOK, NEWPORT (the capital of the island) and WHIPPINGHAM CHURCH, making a stop of 20 minutes to enable visitors to see the church, where QUEEN VICTORIA used to attend Divine Service, when in residence at Osborne. Passing through EAST COWES and OSBORNE ESTATE, we get here the splendid views of STOKES BAY, LEE-ON-SOLENT, GOSPORT and the Home Fleet at anchor. Passing WOOTTON, Portsmouth kennels, QUARR MONASTERY and the ruins of QUARR ABBEY (twelfth century). Proceeding through BINSTEAD into RYDE, through the main streets out to the Esplanade we arrive at the Royal Esplanade Hotel about 12.15, where we make a stop for luncheon. Leaving again at 1.15, we drive the whole length of the Esplanade and from here get a full view of PORTSMOUTH, SPITHEAD, SOUTHSEA, the Forts and the Model Yacht Pond. Continuing through ELMSFIELD and BRADING, we see the old CHURCH, WHIPPING POST and STOCKS, also the BULL RING, ROMAN VILLA, etc. Leaving Brading we drive through SANDOWN into SHANKLIN ; from here we commence to climb to an altitude of 764 feet above sea level, where we get a wonderful view of the English Channel, which we keep in sight for another 15 miles. Passing LUCCOMBE CHINE, we descend to BONCHURCH, one of the prettiest spots on the Island, passing Bonchurch Pond into VENTNOR, where (time permitting) we allow a stop of 20 minutes at the seaside. Leaving Ventnor we pass along the nine miles of the UNDERCLIFF DRIVE to ST. LAWRENCE, NITON and BLACKGANG, where for ruggedness the scenery is equal to any in Europe. Passing CHALE CHURCH we come to the villages of YAFFORD, BRIGHSTONE, MOTTISTONE, BROOK and TAPNELL. From here we see Tennyson's Monument on Afton Downs. Arriving at YARMOUTH ample time is allowed for tea, before catching the boat scheduled to leave at 4.55, which brings us back to Lymington, and we arrive back at the Lansdowne, Bournemouth, at 6.45.

ANOTHER ROYAL BLUE WONDER TOUR.

SIX DAYS' TOUR arranged by Thomas Cook and Son to

DEVON and CORNWALL

# SAFETY FIRST.

Mess.rs ELLIOTT BROS., (Bournemouth) L.TD

Head Booking & Registered Office:- 68, HOLDENHURST RD. BOURNEMOUTH.

## ROYAL ☒ BLUE

SAFETY BOURNEMOUTH FIRST
PULCHRITUDO ET SALUBRITAS

MOTOR COACHES                    & PRIVATE HIRE CARS.

PHONE 1610.

# MOTOR COACH GUIDE.

How to see Bournemouth, the Scenic and Historical Beauty Spots for 100 miles around.

*"Pulchritudo et Salubritas"*

Bournemouth, beautiful and health-giving — The Evergreen Valley — "The Forest City of the South" — The Headquarters of the Royal Blue Magnificent Fleet of

## ALL-WEATHER COACHES.

Telephones: 1610, 1611, 1612, (Private Branch Exchange).

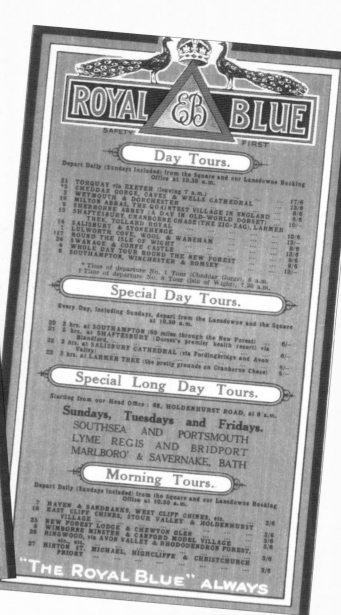

## ROYAL ☒ BLUE
SAFETY FIRST

### Day Tours.

Depart Daily (Sundays Included) from the Square and our Lansdowne Booking Office at 10.30 a.m.

| | | |
|---|---|---|
| 31 | TORQUAY via EXETER (leaving 7 a.m.) | |
| *3 | CHEDDAR GORGE, CAVES & WELLS CATHEDRAL | 17/6 |
| 2 | WEYMOUTH & DORCHESTER | 12/6 |
| 19 | MILTON ABBAS, THE QUAINTEST VILLAGE IN ENGLAND | 8/6 |
| 13 | SHERBORNE ABBEY (A DAY IN OLD-WORLD DORSET) | 8/6 |
| | SHAFTESBURY, CRANBORNE CHASE (THE ZIG-ZAG), LARMER TREE, TOLLARD ROYAL | 10/- |
| 14 | SALISBURY & STONEHENGE | 10/6 |
| *17 | LULWORTH COVE, WOOL & WAREHAM | 12/- |
| 26 | SWANAGE & CORFE CASTLE | 8/6 |
| | ROUND THE ISLE OF WIGHT | 12/6 |
| | WHOLE DAY TOUR ROUND THE NEW FOREST | 8/6 |
| 6 | SOUTHAMPTON, WINCHESTER & ROMSEY | 12/- |

* Time of departure No. 1 Tour (Cheddar Gorge), 8 a.m.
† Time of departure No. 8 Tour (Isle of Wight), 7.30 a.m.

### Special Day Tours.

Every Day, including Sundays, depart from the Lansdowne and the Square at 10.30 a.m.

| | | |
|---|---|---|
| 20 | 5 hrs. at SOUTHAMPTON (60 miles through the New Forest) | |
| 21 | 5 hrs. at SHAFTESBURY (Dorset's premier health resort) via Blandford. | 6/- |
| 22 | 5 hrs. at SALISBURY CATHEDRAL (via Fordingbridge and Avon Valley) | 6/- |
| 23 | 5 hrs. at LARMER TREE (the pretty grounds on Cranborne Chase) | 6/- |

### Special Long Day Tours.

Starting from our Head Office : 68, HOLDENHURST ROAD, at 8 a.m.

**Sundays, Tuesdays and Fridays.**

SOUTHSEA AND PORTSMOUTH
LYME REGIS AND BRIDPORT
MARLBORO' & SAVERNAKE, BATH

### Morning Tours.

Depart Daily (Sundays included) from the Square and our Lansdowne Booking Office at 10.30 a.m.

| | | |
|---|---|---|
| 7 | HAVEN & SANDBANKS, WEST CLIFF CHINES, etc. | |
| 18 | EAST CLIFF CHINES, STOUR VALLEY & HOLDENHURST VILLAGE | 2/6 |
| 25 | NEW FOREST LODGE & CHEWTON GLEN | 3/6 |
| 8 | WIMBORNE MINSTER & CANFORD MODEL VILLAGE | 3/6 |
| 26 | RINGWOOD, via AVON VALLEY & RHODODENDRON FOREST, etc., etc. | 3/6 |
| 27 | HINTON ST. MICHAEL, HIGHCLIFFE & CHRISTCHURCH PRIORY | 3/6 |

## "THE ROYAL BLUE" ALWAYS

## SWANAGE & CORFE CASTLE.

Depart Daily Lansdowne and Square, 10.30 a.m.            Return Fare 8/6

PASSING POOLE, the route lies through the TICHBORNE ESTATES, Upton House being at one time the Dorsetshire seat of Sir Roger Tichborne. Passing through LYTCHETT MINSTER, the seat of the late Sir Eliot Lees, we arrive quite near the immense cordite factory at HOLTON HEATH, known as one of the "hush" factories erected by the Government in the early part of the Great War. Passing through the old Saxon town of WAREHAM, we cross the river Frome. After another spin of about five miles, across the "Isle of Purbeck," we reach the quaintest of Dorset's former "towns," CORFE CASTLE. The castle is situated in an opening which divides the Purbeck range. The history of the castle is long and eventful. The first mention dates as far back as 978, when Edward King of West Saxons, was barbarously murdered by his stepmother Elfrida. The major portion of the old ruins dates from the Norman period, although there still exists some very fine zig-zag masonry of the Saxon period. Its ruinous condition to-day is attributed to Oliver Cromwell, who after besieging and capturing the castle, ordered it to be destroyed by gunpowder.
PURBECK HILLS, embracing charming views of Swanage Bay and the English Channel, running through the stone quarrying district of LANGTON MATRAVERS, and reaching SWANAGE, a growing seaside resort, said by Charles Kingsley years ago that all it only wanted houses to make it famous. Well, it has got the houses now! Its development can be chiefly attributed to the efforts of its two natives, the great London contractors, Mowlem and Burt. Numerous pieces of old London can be seen, including the facade of the Town Hall, which came from the Mercers' Company and is Wren's work, also remnants of the Albert Memorial Hall, Billingsgate Market, etc. Many of the lamp posts bear the inscription "St. George's," Hanover Square," or "G.R. IV." Time will be allowed to visit the GREAT GLOBE, an exact representation of the earth in Portland stone, weighing 40 tons and 10 feet in diameter; also the famous TILLY WHIM CAVES, etc. The return journey will be made via CORFE CASTLE, where tea can be obtained at the Bankes Hotel.

## BEKYNTON CAFÉ
### WELLS.

*Hot and Cold Luncheons. Teas. Ices. Sundaes. Ice Bricks.*

## LULWORTH COVE.

Depart Daily, LANSDOWNE and SQUARE, at 10.30 a.m.            Return Fare 8/6

THIS journey is by LYTCHETT MINSTER, interesting for its inn sign, Peter's Finger, the historic town of WAREHAM, STOBOROUGH and the lovely avenue, HOLME LANE. The view from the Rifle Range across to the Purbeck Hills is very striking, through the main camp of the famous Tank Corps over the heaths of the Isle of Purbeck, underneath the Purbeck Range through EAST LULWORTH, a pretty Dorset village set in a little from the sea-gap of Arish Mell, under the shelter of Lulworth Castle for generations the home of the Weld family. Reaching LULWORTH COVE, lunch or tea will be in readiness, time being allowed to visit the picturesque cove and obtain charming views of Weymouth Bay, Portland, etc. The rock scenery of Lulworth Cove, Stair Hole, St. Oswald's Bay, Man o' War Cove, Durdle Door, and westwards towards the Nothe Point is without doubt the most striking and beautiful along the English coast. Few places are more interesting geologically for so great a variety of rocks and rock structure. The return journey is up hill and down into WOOL and affords magnificent views over the greater part of Dorset, passing "Welbridge" Manor House, the scene of "Tess's Wedding Night" in Thomas Hardy's story "Tess of the D'Urbervilles." Also associated with Hardy's "Tess" is Bindon Abbey, a little way off.

## THE COVE HOTEL & RESTAURANT
### LULWORTH COVE.
Telephone West Lulworth 3

Seating Accommodation for about 500.                Park for 100 Cars.
Proprietors: F. A. Oaten, W. J. McCabe.

Tourist Motor Coaches (Southampton) Ltd. Thomas Tilling Ltd had begun negotiations for the take over of Tourist in November 1934, courtesy of a tip-off from William Wells Graham of Hants & Dorset. Southern National was again chosen to make the initial purchase — from Tilling this time — of £46,139 0s 8d. As before, the express operations went to Southern/Western National, and the excursions and routes to Hants & Dorset; a 36-strong fleet of motor coaches was split three ways. In addition the Grosvenor Square/Bedford Place property (known as the Tourist Motor Station) in Southampton was sold by Southern National to Hants & Dorset, for £25,000.

Southern/Western National forthwith subsumed the 'Tourist' identity under that of Royal Blue (which they retained for their express work), but Hants & Dorset displayed both 'Royal Blue' and 'Tourist' upon its coaches until 1946. The National companies retained just three lock-up shops in Southampton — at Six Dials, Northam.

Tourist had been founded by Bertie H. Ransom at Back-of-the-Walls, Southampton, in 1919. His express service to London owed its origin to the General Strike in 1926 — he ran back and forth with otherwise stranded ships' passengers from Southampton Docks. On 7 November 1927 Ransom had joined forces with S. C. Bullock and Thomas Briggs, newly arrived in the area, having sold their Lancashire interests to Ribble Motor Services Ltd. At the same time W. Aloisius Browne's Hiawatha & Queen Services (more recently Hiawatha Motor Coaches) was purchased together with an express run of sorts to London and premises in Winchester Road, Southampton, which the reconstituted Tourist Motor Coaches (Southampton) Ltd used as a site for a large garage and maintenance headquarters. The new Tourist had then set out to operate express services additionally to Bournemouth, Exeter and Plymouth and, northward, to Oxford, Stratford-upon-Avon, Lichfield, Newcastle-under-Lyme, Warrington and Liverpool, the last for the benefit of members of the shipping industry. Thus it was that Southern/Western National's version of Royal Blue first gained running rights to far-flung Merseyside.

One additional treasure gained by SN/WN at this time was Elliott Bros' former Traffic Manager, Clement Preece, who with his new employers became Traffic Superintendent (Express Services), based at Exeter. The personality, wit and charm of this man comes across strongly in his entertaining account of life in the industry (*Wheels to the West*, 1974). He was to rise to the rank of Traffic Manager (Commercial) during World War 2 and came to be known affectionately as 'Mr Royal Blue'. He was also a keen and gifted photographer, and many of the finely composed publicity pictures of Royal Blue vehicles at work in the 1960s are his.

Also inherited from Elliott Bros was its membership of Associated Motorways — a co-ordinating scheme centred upon St Margaret's Coach Station in Cheltenham, the home of Black & White Motorways Ltd (jointly owned by Bristol Tramways & Carriage Co Ltd, Midland Red and the City of Oxford Motor Services Ltd). Associated Motorways was formed in July 1934 and also included in its original form Red & White and United Counties. John Hibbs succinctly described it (1968) as 'a partnership … whereby each member has contributed certain specified services to the pool and has agreed that they shall be operated together as part of a single operation'. Elliott Bros had transferred seven of its routes to the scheme and had found that this resulted in a welcome saving, as revenue allocated upon a mileage basis gained considerable economies (as the Elliotts had also discovered in their pooling scheme with Southern/Western National). All the participant coaches ran in their owners' colours, although publicity material featured a coach in a non-existent orange and green livery. A geographically centred passenger-exchange point (at Cheltenham) was thus established for the Midlands, South Wales and the South West

John Elliott of Royal Blue was seeking alternatives in 1933, whilst helping set up Associated Motorways.

*Above:* When Elliott Bros' Royal Blue fleet was divided three ways between Southern National, Western National and Hants & Dorset in 1935 this beautiful normal-control ADC 424 coach (RU 6728) was actually acquired by the last of the trio. However, Southern National and Western National received nine identical examples apiece, the majority with Duple bodies, the rest Hall Lewis. *Colin Morris collection*

The Tourist operation at Southampton was started by Bertie Ransom in 1919. It was beefed up considerably following the arrival from Lancashire of S. C. Bullock and Thomas Briggs in 1927, when Tourist Coaches (Southampton) Ltd was formed. By 1933 it was operating a fleet of five Chevrolets, 18 Leylands, 12 Albions and three Studebakers. This Tourist Albion PR28/Strachans 26-seater (TR 6334) became No 3522 in the Western National fleet. *Colin Morris collection*

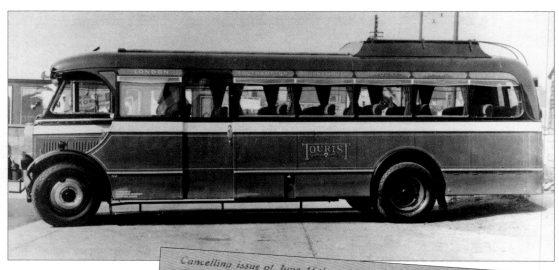

*Right:* In May 1935 Tilling followed up the purchase of Elliott Bros (Bournemouth) Ltd by acquiring the Southampton-based operations of Tourist Coaches (Southampton) Ltd. The fleet was divided among Southern/Western National and Hants & Dorset Motor Services. One of the three Albion PV70/Strachans coaches involved went to Southern National as No 3534 (OW 1879) but did not join the Royal Blue fleet.
*Alan Lambert collection*

## TOURIST
MOTOR COACHES

'Phones 4848 and 4046.
## REGULAR DAILY SERVICES TO
# LONDON
### COSY, CENTRAL-HEATED COACHES.

| FROM SOUTHAMPTON | FROM LONDON |
|---|---|
| 7.30 a.m. via Winchester and Guildford | 9.15 a.m. via Basingstoke & Winchester |
| 8.30 a.m. via Winchester & Basingstoke | 12.0 noon (Sats. only) via Guildford & Winchester |
| *9.0 a.m. via Eastleigh Bishop's Waltham and Guildford | 2.0 p.m. via Basingstoke & Winchester |
| 10.30 a.m. via Eastleigh, Winchester and Basingstoke | *6.0 via Guildford, Bishop's Waltham and Eastleigh |
| 12.0 (Sats. only) via Winchester & Guildford | 6.30 p.m. via Basingstoke & Winchester |
| 2.0 p.m. via Winchester and Basingstoke | 7.30 p.m. via Guildford Winchester and Eastleigh |
| 6.0 via Winchester & Basingstoke | 11.30 p.m. via Basingstoke, Winchest' |

*Weds. and Sats. only.

| Single | Day Return | Period |
|---|---|---|
| 5/6 | 7/- | 10/- |

### CHEAP EXCURSIONS (daily)
on our 7.30 and 8.30 Services to
# LONDON Return 6/-
Available to return by any of our services same day

WEDNESDAYS and SUNDAYS at 11.30 a.m
BASINGSTOKE ............... 4/6 Return
SUNDAY at 8.30 a.m.
BATH and BRISTOL ............... 6/6

# BOURNEMOUTH TWICE DAILY
10.15 a.m., 1.30 p.m.,
Returning 12 noon, 4.30 p.m.,
3/-, Single; 4/- Day Return; 5/- Period

SEATS MAY BE BOOKED AT
Our Booking Offices: 171, St. Mary's Road (Six Dials), and 59, Above Bar; Dolphin Hotel; Crown Hotel, Shirley; and usual Tourist Agents.
LONDON AGENTS: Thomas Transport, 12, Villiers Street (Charing Cross). Telephone. 4526 Gerrard.
Travel by Tourist for the best service. Superior to all others.

Cancelling issue of June 16th                    Next Issue June 3rd.

1934/5 Winter Service                    Commencing Jan. 1st

THE SYMBOL OF SAFETY
The SOUTHERN NATIONAL OMNIBUS CO., Ltd.
The WESTERN NATIONAL OMNIBUS CO., Ltd.
PROPRIETORS OF
ROYAL BLUE SERVICES

ROUTE "A"  7 Services each way Daily 7    TABLE 2
# London, Southampton, Bournemouth & Poole
WITH CONNECTIONS TO & FROM THE ISLE OF WIGHT
via Basingstoke : Winchester  or  via Guildford : Winchester
Lyndhurst                              Romsey

## ROUTES LONDON AND WEST OF ENGLAND

Reference
MAIN ROUTE VIA BASINGSTOKE
MAIN ROUTE VIA GUILDFORD
DIRECT CONNECTIONS
OTHER SERVICES

Through Services are maintained daily—winter and summer—at various departure times along the routes depicted above, serving the South & West of England.

THE WESTERN NATIONAL OMNIBUS CO., Ltd., 48/50, Queen Street, Exeter.
ROYAL BLUE SERVICES, The Square Station, Bournemouth. Phone 2182.
THE SOUTHERN NATIONAL OMNIBUS CO., Ltd., 48/52, Queen Street, Exeter. Phone 6187.

1,000 15/4/35

of England — and Southern/Western National's Royal Blue was now an important contributor to that network.

The 'Royal Blue' identity was now applied to Southern National express-service coaches from London to Swanage and Weymouth (Dorset) and to Ilfracombe and Lynton (Devon), as well as to Western National's to Minehead (Somerset) and to Newquay and Penzance (Cornwall), replacing green-liveried vehicles upon such duties. As Elliott Bros (Bournemouth) Ltd had not run express services west of Devon, routes to Bude, St Ives and Penzance took Royal Blue express services for the first time into Cornwall, a county not served by the Associated Motorways network.

Although ex-Elliott vehicles continued to be employed at the outset, Southern/Western National's new Bristol JJW chassis for Royal Blue were bodied to a standard 32-seat pattern by Eastern Counties, Beadle and Weymann. Although from a design point of view there was a strong family resemblance to SN/WN saloon-bus bodywork of

the later 1930s a subtle difference went beyond the obvious 'dark blue for green' and a large roof pannier on the express coaches of Royal Blue. Whereas the cream waistband on the service buses ended at the rear in either a wrap-around or a fishtail, that upon the Royal Blue coaches terminated in a distinct arrowhead. Someone with a keen æsthetic sensibility — most likely Clement Preece — had been at work on the drawing board. This design was applied to further new Bristol coaches and was utilised to rebody some earlier vehicles, including Leyland Tigers. In 1937, 16 new AEC Regal chassis were similarly bodied — eight for Southern National, built by Duple, and the rest, for Western National, by the Plymouth-based firm of W. Mumford. By the outbreak of World War 2 there were 88 vehicles on the road in this standard style.

In 1937 a series of 'Royal Blue inclusive Holidays' was launched in conjunction with selected express-service destinations, together with four new non-stop services from London: the Channel Coast Express (to Bournemouth) and Weymouth Bay

In preparation for a distinguished new 'Royal Blue' image the Southern/Western National companies agreed upon a new standard coachwork design to be fitted to 28 Bristol JJW chassis, the contracts going to Eastern Counties, Beadle and Weymann. Each builder's handywork was divided equally between the two companies. Eastern Counties-bodied No 163 (BTA 453) went to Western National. *Alan Lambert collection*

Whilst several livery and logo variations were tried out on the Eastern Counties batch (W. J. Iden would have approved, had he still been there), those coaches produced by the other two coachbuilders had settled into a largely dark-blue design which adopted the winged wheel device incorporating the company name. No 188 (ATT 938), by Weymann, was an example. *Alan Lambert collection*

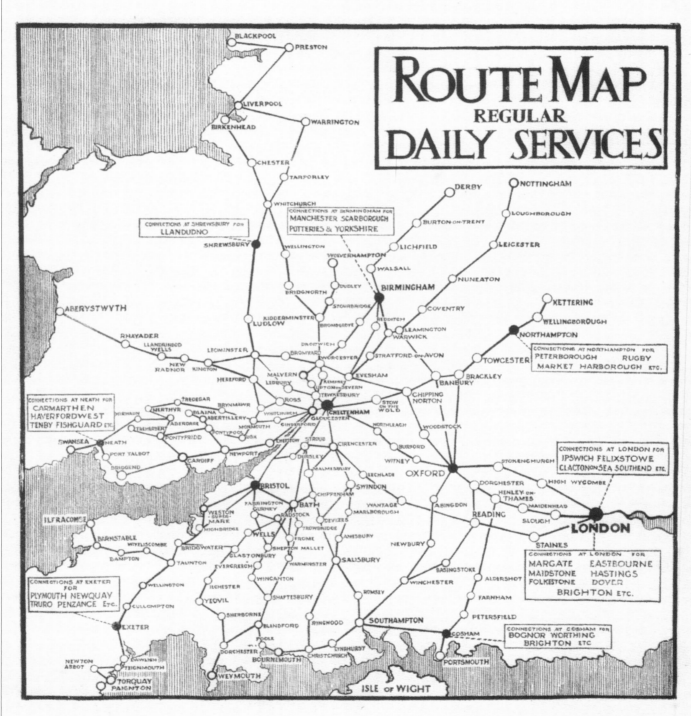

# Royal Blue — Southdown — East Kent

## NATIONAL JOINT SERVICES

### BOURNEMOUTH, PORTSMOUTH, BRIGHTON
### EASTBOURNE, HASTINGS, DOVER, DEAL, MARGATE

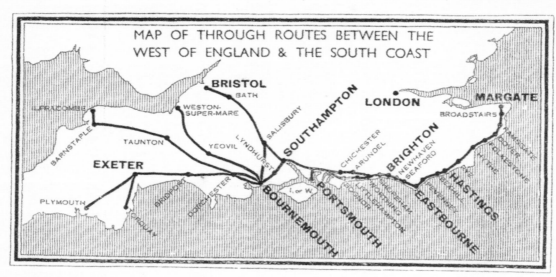

MAP OF THROUGH ROUTES BETWEEN THE WEST OF ENGLAND & THE SOUTH COAST

| UP. | a.m. | a.m. | noon | p.m. | p.m. | p.m. | p.m. | p.m. |
|---|---|---|---|---|---|---|---|---|
| Bournemouth | 8.00 | 10.15 | 12.00 | 2.45 | 3.30 | 5.15 | 8.15 | —— |
| Southampton | 9.29 | 11.44 | 1.29 | 4.14 | 4.58 | 6.44 | 9.44 | —— |
| Portsmouth | 10.40 | 12.55 | 2.40 | 5.25 | 6.10 | 7.55 | 10.55 | —— |
| Brighton | 1.28 | 3.58 | 5.28 | —— | 8.58 | —— | —— | —— |
| Eastbourne | 3.04 | 5.35 | 7.04 | —— | —— | —— | —— | —— |
| Hastings | 4.00 | 6.30 | 8.00 | —— | —— | —— | —— | —— |
| Folkestone | 6.36 | 8.36 | —— | —— | —— | —— | —— | —— |
| Dover | 6.57 | —— | —— | —— | —— | —— | —— | —— |
| Ramsgate | 8.05 | —— | —— | —— | —— | —— | —— | —— |
| Margate | 8.25 | —— | —— | —— | —— | —— | —— | —— |
| DOWN. | a.m. | a.m. | a.m. | a.m. | a.m. | a.m. | a.m. | a.m. |
| Margate | —— | —— | —— | —— | —— | 8.15 | 10.45 | —— |
| Ramsgate | —— | —— | —— | —— | —— | 8.35 | 11.05 | —— |
| Dover | —— | —— | —— | —— | —— | 9.43 | 12.13 | —— |
| Folkestone | —— | —— | —— | —— | 9.00 | 10.05 | 12.35 | 3.45 |
| Hastings | —— | —— | —— | 8.30 | 11.00 | 12.04 | 3.04 | 5.34 |
| Eastbourne | —— | —— | —— | 9.19 | 11.49 | 12.54 | 4.04 | 6.54 |
| Brighton | —— | —— | 9.00 | 10.25 | 1.05 | 2.44 | 5.10 | 8.00 |
| Portsmouth | 8.10 | 10.45 | 11.45 | 1.45 | 4.45 | 6.00 | 8.30 | —— |
| Southampton | 9.16 | 11.51 | 12.51 | 2.51 | 5.51 | 7.06 | 9.36 | —— |
| Bournemouth | 10.50 | 1.25 | 2.25 | 4.25 | 7.25 | 8.40 | 11.10 | —— |

FARES.

Bournemouth and :—

| | S. | DR. | PR. |
|---|---|---|---|
| Portsmouth | 5/- | 7/- | 8/- |
| Brighton | 9/6 | 10/6 | 15/- |
| Eastbourne | 11/6 | —— | 20/- |
| Hastings | 12/6 | —— | 21/6 |
| Folkestone | 15/6 | —— | 25/6 |
| Dover | 16/- | —— | 26/6 |
| Ramsgate | 18/- | —— | 30/- |
| Margate | 18/6 | —— | 30/- |

THE POOLE
FEEDER SERVICE
CONNECTS WITH
ALL SERVICES
AT
BOURNEMOUTH

*Connections available at Portsmouth to Littlehampton and Bognor see Time Table F10.*

---

ROYAL BLUE
BLACK and WHITE
GREYHOUND

# Associated Motorways

MIDLAND RED
UNITED COUNTIES
RED and WHITE

## BOURNEMOUTH, NEWBURY, READING
## OXFORD, BIRMINGHAM

| | READ DOWN | | READ UP | | FARES | | | |
|---|---|---|---|---|---|---|---|---|
| | a.m. | a.m. | | | From Bournemouth to : | S | DR | PR |
| Bournemouth | 10.30 | 9.45 | 5.30 | 6.31 | | | | |
| Newbury | 2.10 | —— | 2.22 | —— | Newbury | 6/6 | —— | 9/9 |
| Reading | —— | 1.54 | —— | 2.35 | Reading | 6/6 | 8/3 | 9/9 |
| Oxford | 3.21 | 3.21 | 1.12 | 1.17 | Oxford | 9/- | —— | 15/6 |
| Birmingham | 6.5 | 6.35 | 9.30 | 9.30 | Birmingham | 13/6 | —— | 23/- |

IT'S CHEAPER BY COACH !

5

*Right:* The same basic body design, but with forward entrance, was chosen in 1937 for 16 AEC Regal chassis. No 1061 (ETA 995) was one of eight for Southern National built by Duple; those for Western National were constructed by W. Mumford of Plymouth. Positioning the door at the front meant that an eye-catching taper could now form part of the rear wing. *The Omnibus Society / Alan Lambert collection*

*Right:* Much pleased with their standard Royal Blue coachwork design, the two companies decided to rebody some of their more sprightly vehicles from earlier years. In addition to some ADC and AEC chassis ex Elliott, their own Leyland Tiger chassis were similarly favoured. No 3140 (DR 8638) was a TS1 model of 1931. *A. Jones / London Trolleybus Preservation Society*

*Left:* No 460 (CTA 548) was one of six Bedford WTB coaches taken into stock by Southern National in 1937 which were dressed in the red and cream livery of Scarlet Pimpernel, the Ilfracombe firm acquired the previous year. Pictured at Bideford, this vehicle and its fellow WTBs were quite likely to be called upon to make express runs to London at weekends. *The Omnibus Society*

Express in Southern National territory and the Minehead Express and Cornish Coast Express by Western National. In connection with the South Coast Express (joint with Southdown and East Kent) a Royal Blue sub-station was set up at Southdown's Hilsea depot, to aid services starting from that company's garage in Hyde Park Road, Portsmouth.

The declaration of war in September 1939 saw a great deal of additional traffic, not just of London schoolchildren evacuated to the West Country but of adults who responded periodically to enemy threats, perceived or actual. The Hilsea sub-depot gained considerable importance that very month, when the South Coast Express east of Portsea Island was withdrawn for the duration of hostilities, together with 10 other express services across Royal Blue territory.

In September 1942, in order to conserve fuel supplies, all operators were ordered to cease express coach working completely. The ever-alert Clem Preece came up with a solution which kept the Royal Blue flag flying, whereby some two dozen Royal Blue coaches worked six limited-stop stage-carriage services — for 'service personnel and war workers' — centred upon Bournemouth:

400  Bournemouth–New Milton–Southampton;
401  Southampton–Titchfield–Fareham–
      Portsmouth;
402  Bournemouth–Bridport–Exeter;
403  Bournemouth–Sherborne–Yeovil;
404  Honiton–Yeovil–Shaftesbury;
405  Bournemouth–Shaftesbury–Trowbridge.

The rest of the Royal Blue fleet was relegated to running as relief vehicles on stage-carriage duties, some of them towing gas trailers. The 405 route was supplemented from the outset by standard (green) stage-carriage saloon buses, which simply kept going when the other five 'emergency

services' ceased at the war's end, with no reciprocal running rights for Hants & Dorset, and it took the latter four years of quiet diplomacy to bring to an end this continuing stage-carriage intrusion into its territory.

Postwar, streamlined Beadle-bodied Bristol L and LL coaches began to replace the earlier and rebodied coaches in the Royal Blue fleet. By now Clement Attlee's Labour Government had nationalised the railways and subsumed the Tilling-controlled bus companies under the British Transport Commission. Thus when, in 1952, Royal Blue's first full-fronted (Bristol LS) coaches arrived they were bodied by Eastern Coach Works — now drawn, like Bristol, further under the BTC's 'Tilling Association' control. Whilst Southern National remained an active operational company (until 31 December 1969) all new Royal Blue coaches entering service were built by the Bristol/ECW manufacturing duet.

In 1942 virtually every express service in the UK was brought to an ordered halt in order to preserve fuel for the war effort. That September the Royal Blue fleet ceased running on all save six routes, converted to limited-stop stage-carriage services. AEC Regal No 1057 (ETA 983) is here disguised as a service bus on route 405 (Trowbridge–Shaftesbury–Bournemouth). Presumably Western National thought its contribution should be painted green. It became known jocularly as 'the Green Linnet'. *S. L. Poole*

In 1951 Southern National/Western National shared equally a delivery of 24 'stretched' examples of the Bristol L6B — the LL6B. The result was an even more elegant version of an already classic Royal Blue coach. The recently sanctioned extra length meant that a few additional passengers — up to a total of 37 — could be accommodated. Preserved No 1250 (LTA 729) shows off its handsome curvaceous lines. *Colin Morris collection*

*Right:* Southern National's very presentable Bristol LL6B coaches, with their luxurious 37-seat Duple coachwork, made most acceptable substitutes for Royal Blue coaches and, following their introduction in 1951, were regularly the first vehicles to be drafted in for relief work. Here No 1323 (LTA 902) has paused at Southdown's Hilsea depot before continuing south to Hyde Park Road to collect its passengers. *Alan Lambert*

*Right:* A directive from above seems to have gone out to the Tilling Association's subsidiaries in 1958 to the effect that it would be nice if individual company coach liveries could be reduced to basic livery below the waistrail, with cream above — the æsthetic powers of the 'top brass' seem to have been on the wane. Bristol LL6B/Duple No 1277 is now a 'cream top', as drivers called them briefly. *Alan Lambert*

*Right:* There were occasions when summer-Saturday demands upon Royal Blue were so heavy that desperate regulators at either end of an express route grabbed whatever they could to shift all the passengers. Sometimes an independent's coach was called up at the last minute, but on this occasion it was a humble Bristol LS5G saloon of Southern National that 'popped up' to Victoria — with 45 rather-less-than-comfortable seats. *M. Page*

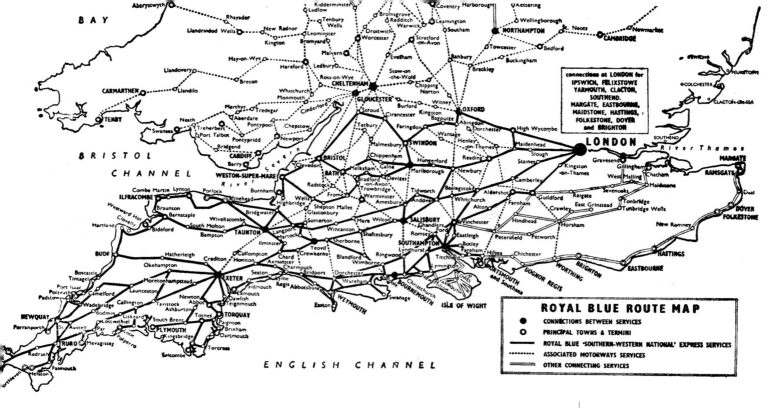

ROYAL BLUE ROUTE MAP

● CONNECTIONS BETWEEN SERVICES
○ PRINCIPAL TOWNS & TERMINI
— ROYAL BLUE 'SOUTHERN-WESTERN NATIONAL' EXPRESS SERVICES
······ ASSOCIATED MOTORWAYS SERVICES
══ OTHER CONNECTING SERVICES

connections at LONDON for IPSWICH, FELIXSTOWE YARMOUTH, CLACTON, SOUTHEND, MARGATE, EASTBOURNE, MAIDSTONE, HASTINGS, FOLKESTONE, DOVER and BRIGHTON

*Left:* A typical Saturday Associated Motorways working for a Southern National Bristol LS6G/ECW 41-seat coach on express relief duty. No 1371 (OTT 80) departs Bristol Omnibus Co's Wells depot *en route* to Cheltenham in the autumn of 1969. *DWR Picture Library*

*Left:* The classic Southern National badge, derived from the original Royal Blue logo introduced in 1935. It sat well inside this dished device designed for use upon Bristol LS and MW coaches of the 1950s and '60s. *Mike J. Stephens*

*Right:* Royal Blue Bristol MW6G/ECW coach No 2221 (XUO 731) departs Plymouth for points west in September 1969. Bristol MW (Medium Weight) coaches had first entered service with Southern/Western National in 1958. *DWR Picture Library*

*Below:* From time to time, when not needed for express work, Royal Blue coaches sometimes — and to passengers' surprise — turned up on private hires. Here Bristol LS5G No 2212 (VDV 775) has arrived in the delightful resort of Lyme Regis in the autumn of 1969. *DWR Picture Library*

SOUTHERN NATIONAL OMNIBUS COMPANY

*Left:* Bristol MWG No 2270 (253 KTA), delivered in 1962, was one of a batch of 15 39-seaters bodied by ECW for service with Royal Blue. However, just two years later, although the whole batch remained in dark blue and cream, four were re-labelled 'Southern National' and the rest 'Western National'. The vehicle is pictured 'going west' against a backdrop of the kind of 'West Country' which attracted all those tourists. *Ian Allan Library*

*Lower left:* Dramatically lit, semi-retired Bristol L5G No 372 (GTA 394) has found a less strenuous role as an express-service passenger waiting room at Bridgwater bus station in 1967. Originally built (in 1942) with a Strachans body, it was lengthened to LL5G standard and rebodied by ECW in 1954. *DWR Picture Library*

*Below:* Operating as an express-service relief vehicle, No 434 (186 KTA) takes the centre line as it sweeps along the Bagshot bypass (in Surrey) with the 08.30 from Victoria to Lynton. This tidy little 33-seater was a 1962 Bristol SUL4A with ECW coach body. *Mike J. Stephens*

*Above:* Technically 'on hire' to Royal Blue on yet another Saturday, Bristol SUL4A/ECW 33-seat coach No 428 (278 KTA) — a Western National vehicle — was *en route* from Lynton to Taunton for a connection to Bristol when photographed in August 1969. *DWR Picture Library*

*Right:* Express services were, of course, run on an all-year-round basis, but traffic increased considerably during holiday peak periods. At such times many vehicles were hired from other operators for relief work, local Tilling companies taking pride of place. Here a pair of newly delivered Wilts & Dorset Bristol MW6G/ECW 41-seaters — Nos 725/6 (EMR 300/1D), with passengers already aboard — await departure from Salisbury coach station on 16 July 1966. *G. Ridler*

*Right:* Pictured at the Radipole, Weymouth, garage previously occupied by Road Motors Ltd, followed by the NO&T, is No 1419 (EDV 549D), a 1966 Bristol MW6G/ECW coach in Royal Blue livery, which enabled it to double as an express coach when required. *DWR Picture Library*

*Left:* What turned out to be the swansong for the Royal Blue coaches operated nominally by the Southern National Omnibus Co Ltd began in 1964 with the purchase of the impressive Bristol RELH. Built to the newly permitted 36ft length, these coaches, with rear-mounted Gardner engines and ECW bodywork, could seat 45 in considerable comfort. No 2365 (HDV 624E) was one of a pair delivered to Southern National in 1967. *Alan Lambert*

Bristol RELH6G/ECW 45-seater 2358 (ATA 102B), a Western National vehicle, stands proud amid the MWs at Bournemouth's Rutland Road garage. The garage was originally the property of Elliott Bros and came into SN/WN hands with the purchase of that firm in 1935. *DWR Picture Library*

The National Bus Company did its very best to introduce a charming historical note to the 'centenary' by taking the trouble to hire this four-in-hand coach from the Dodington Coach Museum in Gloucestershire, together with Colin Henderson, the curator, as driver. With 'Royal Blue' nameplates and some blue paint added, it ran from Holmsley to Bournemouth in celebration of the day Thomas Elliott got his first licence to drive a cab. 'Royal Blue' came later! *Ian Allan Library*

## Bibliography

Sources found to be helpful in the compilation of this volume and/or recommended for further reading are:

*Books*
Crawley, R. J., MacGregor, D. R., and Simpson, F. D.: *The Years Between — 1909-1969, Vol 1: The National Story to 1929*, (D. R. MacGregor, 1979)
Crawley, R. J., and Simpson, F. D.: *The Years Between — 1909-1969, Vol 3: The Story of Western National and Southern National from 1929* (Calton Promotions, Exeter, 1990)
Cummings, John: *Railway Motor Buses and Bus Services in the British Isles 1902-1933* Vol 2 (OPC, 1980)
Darwin, Bernard: *War on the Line* (Southern Railway Co, 1946)
Delahoy, Richard: *Glory Days: Eastern National* (Ian Allan, 2003)
Gentry, P. W.: *Tramways of the West of England* (LRTL, 1952-60)
Hibbs, John: *The History of British Bus Services* (David & Charles, Newton Abbot, 1968)
Jackson, B. L.: *Isle of Portland Railways* Vol 3 (The Oakwood Press, Usk, 2000)
Morris, Colin: *Hants & Dorset — a history* (DTS Publishing Ltd, Croydon, 1996)
Morris, Colin: *Glory Days: Royal Blue* (Ian Allan, 2000)
Morris, Colin: *Glory Days: Devon General* (Ian Allan, 2006)
Morris, Colin, and Waller, Andrew: *Wilts & Dorset Motor Services Ltd 1915-1972* (Hobnob Press, Salisbury, 2006)
Preece, Clem: *Wheels to the West* (Travel & Transport Ltd, 1974)
Woodworth, Frank: *Victoria Coach Station: The First Fifty Years — 1932-82* (Rochester Press, 1982)

*Journals*
Numerous Articles in *The Engineer, Motor Traction, Motor Transport, Tramway & Railway World, Commercial Motor, Motor Transport Year Book & Directory, Buses Illustrated* and *Buses.*

*Website*
WHOTT: www.busmuseum.org.uk

Readers wishing to learn more about independent operators in the Southern National areas or in other parts of the West Country are referred to a series of booklets published by Roger Grimley, details of which can be obtained from: Old Post, Bigbury, Kingsbridge, Devon, TQ7 4AP.